ISBN 978-1-330-63759-3
PIBN 10085778

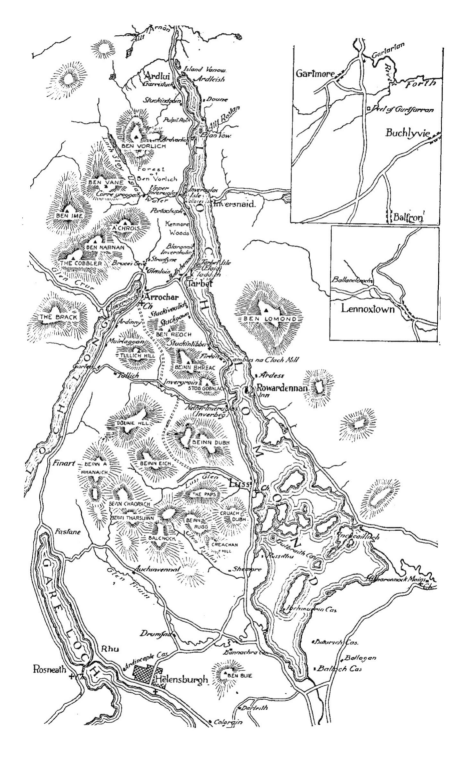

MAP OF LOCH **LOMOND** AND ENVIRON**S**, SHOWING MACFARLANE **LOCATIONS**.

HISTORY OF CLAN MACFARLANE

HISTORY

OF

CLAN MACFARLANE

By

JAMES MACFARLANE

Author of "The Red Fox"

Published under the auspices of the Clan MacFarlane Society,
205 Hope Street, Glasgow

GLASGOW
DAVID J. CLARK LIMITED, 92 UNION STREET
1922

CHIEFS OF MACFARLANE.

1225-1866.

1.—GILCHRIST,	- - - - - - - -	1225-1263*
2.—DUNCAN,	- - - - - - - -	1284-1296*
3.—MALDUIN,	- - - - - - - -	- 1314*
4.—PARLAN,	- - - - - - - -	- 1329*
5.—MALCOLM,	- - - - - - - -	1344-1373*
6.—DUNCAN,	- - - - - - - -	1395-1406*
7.—JOHN, -	- - - - - - - -	1426-1441*
8.—DUNCAN,	- - - - - - - -	1441-
9.—WALTER,	- - - - - - - -	-1488
10.—ANDREW,	- - - - - - - -	1488-1493
11.—SIR JOHN,	- - - - - - - -	-1514
12.—ANDREW,	- - - - - - - -	1514-1544
13.—DUNCAN,	- - - - - - - -	1544-1547
14.—ANDREW,	- - - - - - - -	1547-1612
15.—JOHN, -	- - - - - - - -	1612-1624
16.—WALTER,	- - - - - - - -	1624-1664
17.—JOHN, -	- - - - - - - -	1664-1679
18.—ANDREW,	- - - - - - - -	1679-1685
19.—JOHN, -	- - - - - - - -	1685-1705
20.—WALTER,	- - - - - - - -	1705-1767
21.—WILLIAM,	- - - - - - - -	1767-1787
22.—JOHN, -	- - - - - - - -	1787-
23.—WILLIAM,	- - - - - - - -	-1820
24.—WALTER,	- - - - - - - -	1820-1830
25.—WILLIAM,	- - - - - - - -	1830-1866

These dates are approximate.

INDEX

1186804

ILLUSTRATIONS.

PREFACE.

To all members of Cloinn Pharlain, in all parts of the world—Greeting!

In these pages we have endeavoured to provide a work, the need of which has been long apparent, namely, an authoritative book on the Clan.

While the information contained is by no means complete, still we are able to say that this is the most comprehensive history of the MacFarlanes ever produced. The arrangement is such that anyone, so disposed, may continue this labour of love by completing the work of research. He will not be compelled, as was our case, to build from the foundations, for these are here, we think, well and truly laid. It will be gathered from this statement that we regard this book only as a contribution, albeit a substantial one, to the subject, and we cherish a hope that broadcast circulation will have the effect of bringing information to light to fill the blanks of time and circumstance, readily discernible in our pages.

The formation of the Society of the Clan MacFarlane has resulted in bringing together much new material which is here published for the first time, and we gratefully acknowledge assistance ungrudgingly given by members of the families concerned, as well as by friends interested in historical research.

The necessity for the publication of this work has been borne in upon us in many ways. The recurrence of the same name amongst the chiefs, particularly John, has led to endless confusion in the minds of writers who have been unable, or unwilling, to verify their facts. Some of these errors are quaint, some stupid. For example we may give two dealing with the origin of the name Pharlain.

" There were two clans fighting with each other, one of which was wiped out, all but one helpless little child. One of the conquerors had pity on it, and hid it in a cradle till he could not hide it any longer. They asked him where he got the child. He said it came from a ' far land.' They added the ' Mac,' and the little child lived to be the progenitor of the Mac-Farlanes " (or, more plausibly, MacFarlands.—*Editor*).

" My aunt also told me," the writer continues, " that the crest was a full dressed warrior with drawn sword guarding the child in the cradle : hence the motto, ' This I'll defend.' "

Our readers will agree that this is a very pretty fable ; but what are we to think of the following by a contributor under the nom-de-plume " A Fitzallan," from the *Weekly Scotsman* :—

" I have never been satisfied with any given explanation of the origin of the name MacFarlane. I would offer one that has some probability on its side.

" It is well known that the family name of Stewart was Fitz-Alan until they adopted that of their official rank and became Stewarts.

" About this same time, I have read somewhere, a strong body of the Fitz-Alans crossed the Clyde into the Lennox district where they seem to have been well received, and settled upon Loch Lomondside. Their name (pronounced Fe Alan) would readily become Pharlane or Farlan among the Highlanders around them. Their social position is denoted by the Earl of Lennox bestowing his daughter upon their leader in marriage, and on their part they seem to have been strong adherents of these early Earls of Lennox. Being nearly connected with the Stuart Fitz-Alans, acknowledged kinsmen of the Scottish King, the sequence of events seems easily credible. Parlan may be Gaelic for Bartholomew, but was the latter ever in use among the early Celtic races ? "

So far as we can judge, " A Fitz-Alan " has gone astray over the story of Walter de Fassalane, who married the Countess Margaret, daughter of Donald, the sixth Earl of Lennox. There exist grounds for the belief that Walter was a Fitz-Alan Stewart.

A cutting in lighter vein is as follows :—

" They are an enterprising and progressive people in Dunedin, and do things well at all times. It was in Dunedin that an ingenious Ah Sin—there are many Chinese about the Otago diggings—once made a famous attempt to break through the Scottish ' ring.' A road-contract was advertised by a town council, and when all the tenders came in, the lowest—from one Alexander MacFarlane—was selected, and the would-be contractor invited to call and sign the necessary papers. At the appointed time a bland Chinaman appeared and answered to the name. ' But look ye here, man,' said the surprised head of the council, ' yer name's no' Alexander MacFarlane, surely ? ' ' Allitee,' said the Celestial, ' me savee this pidgin—supposee no gottee name belong ' Mac,' no gettee contract ! ' "

But the MacFarlanes—the genuine MacFarlanes— leave their mark everywhere they go. There is a station named MacFarlane on the Cape Government Railway, near Kimberley ; in Canada there is a Mac-Farlane River, while in Shepherd's Bush, London, there is a thoroughfare called MacFarlane Place. A wayfaring clansman finding himself in this street one night very late, is recorded to have remarked, somewhat unsteadily, that he had reached home, and was with difficulty induced to proceed.

In the United States of America there is a MacFar-lane motor car, needless to say, of the highest grade ; and in Texas, a Loch Sloy Post Office.

The supreme claim to greatness for the Clan, however, has been advanced by a Robert MacFarlane of Brooklyn, New Jersey, U.S.A., who, under date 9th February, 1878, wrote in the North American Journal :—

" If we are to credit the Irish annalists, the MacFarlanes may lay claim to Ireland. It is stated in 'The Annals of Ireland' that after the flood the first settlers were Partholanes. As Dunfermline means Partholane, or MacFarlane's .Fort, and is still called 'Dunfarlane' by the old folk, perhaps the first Partholanes landed at Dunfermline and were Kings of Fife."

The imaginative efforts we have given are indicative of the mass of fiction which, for lack of a true historical record, has grown up around the name of MacFarlane, and they provide a sufficient excuse for the appearance of this volume, even if there were not an abundance of other good reasons.

We, as a Clan, desire neither to be unnecessarily praised nor unduly traduced, but owing to the tardy appearance of this work our "unfriends" have had a long rope. The taunts, "cattle thieves" "name your chief," "broken clan," and the like are ill to brook, yet what was to be expected when the origin of these was the tainted source of the historian of the ancient enemy, paid to produce a history of the Clan Colquhoun. Yet, such is poetic justice or the irony of circumstance, that that author stands convicted out of his own work. He was in the habit of employing literary ghosts, and one of these told the truth without being detected, so we have the quaint situation of the ostensible writer lauding the Colquhouns to the clouds and with no epithet severe enough to besmirch the dastardly MacFarlanes, and at the end of the book, in a few pages turned over to an assistant, the cat out of the bag. We confess that the discovery filled us with an unholy joy.

But, now, in chastened mood, we launch this book trembling lest some similar literary fate o'ertakes us. At all events, we can say with hand on heart, that what is set down here is to the best of our knowledge, and to that we can at least pledge our word.

Yours in the bond of clanship,

JAMES MACFARLANE.

CHAPTER I.

THE history and traditions of the Clan MacFarlane are amongst the most romantic and entrancing of the folklore of the Scottish Highlands.

The early history of the Clan is so interlinked with that of the ancient Earls of Lennox, from which it sprung, that the story of one is practically that of the other, until the extinction of the original house of Lennox, in the reign of James I. of Scotland. Similarly, when the title was bestowed upon John Stewart, a close relationship was maintained through almost the entire period of the Darnley sway. The first Chief of MacFarlane was a son of the second Earl of Lennox, and the second Chief cousin and son-in-law of the fourth Earl, while the tenth Chief of MacFarlane was a son-in-law of the first Darnley Earl.

These things are amplified in the historical portion of the work. This chapter, like the *hors d'œuvres* before a feast, is intended only for the tit-bits of clan lore—vagrant trifles to whet the reader's appetite for the more satisfying viands to follow.

Very well, then! The Clan was Farlan, its badge the cranberry, its slogan or cri de guerre, "Loch Sloy," its motto, "This I'll defend," and its banshee, a black goose. The designation of the Chief was Mac-a-Bhairling or MacPharthaloin, *i.e.* MacFarlane of that Ilk.

They occupied the fastnesses of the Arrochar mountains for some six hundred years. The Colquhouns were their traditional enemies, while their friends and allies were " the clan with a name that is nameless by day "—the MacGregors. They were generally not unfriendly with their neighbours to the west, the Campbells. The principal castles or houses of the chiefs were at Ardleish, Inveruglas, Island Vow, and Arrochar.

Along with Clan Donnachaidh (Robertson), the MacFarlanes are said to have been the earliest of the clans to hold their lánds by feudal charter. Robertson and MacFarlane possess another conjoint distinction in that they are the only clans to bear the Royal Crown of Scotland in their crests.

The MacFarlanes of Arrochar, according to the language of the times, were amongst the families of good account in the Lennox, in the period between the 12th and 14th centuries, and took a greater or less share in the important events transacted in that district.

Skene, in asking himself the question—" What is a Highland Clan ? " eliminates all but such families as, in his opinion, were of Gaelic origin.

He reviews the six great maarmarships or baronies of the Highlands—Gallgael, Moray, Ross, Garmoran, Caithness and Ness. " In the Gallgael maarmarship we have," he continues, " the five great clans of Cuinn, Gillevráy, Eachern, Donnachie, and Pharlane." Thus the house is amongst the most ancient.

The name has been variously spelt, from time to time, MacPharlane, MacPharline, MacFarlin, Mac-Farlane, MacFarland, and MacFarlan. The Gaelic rendering is *Parlanach*, from early Irish, Partholan, and in the Hebrew is Bartholomew, " Son of Furrows."

Although it is usual to associate the clan with the Arrochar country, at a comparatively early date they spread further afield. We find sons of chiefs located at Inversnaid, Ardess (at the foot of Ben Lomond), Gartartan (Gartmore) the Mains of Kilmaronock, Ballaggan, Campsie, and at Drumfad and Auchinvenal in Glen Fruin, while at least two branches of the main stem established themselves in Argyllshire. To this day the districts of Menteith and Buchanan teem with MacFarlanes, and the name predominates in the graveyards of Aberfoyle, Gartmore, Balmaha (Buchanan), Inchcaillach, Luss, Ballyhennan (Tarbet), and Arrochar. In the North of Ireland, Newton Stewart, Co. Tyrone, is a centre of the clan, while under other names there are colonies in Banffshire and Aberdeen.

It is stated that the MacFarlanes once owned six large estates besides Arrochar, which, itself, contains 31,000 acres. They intermarried with some of the noblest of the families of Scotland, such as those of Livingstone, Glencairn, Stewart of Ochiltree, and others.

Away up, deep among the everlasting hills, at least five miles over bog and heather from any highway, lies the little mountain tarn of Loch Sloy. Upon its shores the clan were wont to retire in times of stress, and no more impregnable fortress could be desired. Surrounded by high mountains upon every side, save at the lower end, where the Uglas Water leaps over a high parapet of rocks, a handful of daring men could hold the approach against hundreds. No sound but that of the moorfowl disturbs the silence of the sullen lake. Lonely Loch Sloy gave a war-cry to the clan, and, many times and oft, did the sound of it, hurled from stentorian throats, strike terror to the hearts of luckless opponents.

The chiefs exercised all the powers of feudal lords. They possessed the right of pit and gallows, and condemned persons to be hanged on a knoll at Tarbet. The name of this place of execution is Tom na Croich (the gallows hill).

" The Wizard of the North " had a warm corner in his heart for the Clan MacFarlane, as is shown by frequent references to its history and traditions in the Waverley Novels. In " Rob Roy " we have Bailie Nicol Jarvie's laughable speech to Helen MacGregor, when he claims relationship with her after the fight at the pass of Loch Ard.

"I dinna ken," said the undaunted Bailie, "if the kindred has ever been weel redd out to you yet, cousin, but it's ken'd and can be proved my mother Elspeth MacFarlane was the wife of my father Deacon Nicol Jarvie—peace be wi' them baith!—and Elspeth was the daughter o' Parlane Macfarlane at the sheiling o' Loch Sloy. Now this Parlane Macfarlane, as his surviving daughter, Maggie Macfarlane, alias Macnab, wha married Duncan Macnab o' Stuckavrallachan, can testify, stood as near to your guidman, Robert Macgregor, as in the fourth degree of kindred for——"

But here the worthy man was interrupted by the impatient chieftainess, so that what further revelations he would have made are, alas! lost to us.

The moon is proverbially known in some districts as Macfarlane's buat (lantern), because by its light they usually made their depredatory excursions upon the low country. "Their celebrated pibroch, 'Thogail nam bó,'" says Sir Walter, "which is the name of their gathering tune, intimates these practices, the sense being :—

> "We are bound to drive the bullocks,
> All by hollows, hirsts and hillocks,
> Through the sleet and through the rain,
> When the moon is beaming low,
> On frozen lake and hills of snow,
> Bold and heartily we go ;
> And all for little gain."

Sir Walter, in "A Legend of Montrose," inspires the devoted Highlanders of the Great Marquis with the stirring music of the MacFarlane gathering tune, while in his poem, "Cadzow Castle," he refers to

> "Wild MacFarlane's plaided clan."

William Wordsworth, the poet, too, could not resist the glamour of the romance of the Arrochar country. His poem, "The Brownie's Cell," was suggested by a beautiful ruin upon one of the islands of Loch Lomond, a place chosen for the retreat of a solitary individual, from whom this habitation acquired the name of " The Brownie's Cell." In a foreword to " The Brownie," a sequel to " The Brownie's Cell," he writes,

" Upon a small island, not far from the head of Loch Lomond, are some remains of an ancient building, which was for several years the abode of a solitary individual, one of the last survivors of the Clan of MacFarlane, once powerful in that neighbourhood. Passing along the shore opposite this island in the year 1814, the author learned these particulars, and that this person, then living there, had acquired the appellation of " The Brownie."

The island referred to is manifestly Kilean-a-vow, or Eilean-a-bhuth (the island of the shop or store) as it was called later. Probably Wordsworth's poetic imagination invested the trader, prosaic enough, we daresay, with supernatural attributes, on account of his novel system of shopkeeping. But he has done more and worse than that, for he has permitted himself to believe that, like Adam and Eve from Eden, the MacFarlanes were dispossessed as a punishment for their manifold crimes.

We append those verses of the poem, which deal with the indictment and punishment of this wicked clan.

IV.

Proud remnant was he of a fearless race,
Who stood and flourished face to face
With their perennial hills, but Crime,
Hastening the stern decrees of Time,
Brought low a Power, which from its home
Burst, when repose grew wearisome ;
And, taking impulse from the sword,
And, mocking its own plighted word,
Had found, in ravage widely dealt,
It's warfare's crown, its travel's belt !

V.

All, all were dispossessed, save him whose smile
Shot lightning through this lone isle !
No right had he but what he made
To this small spot, his leafy shade ;
But the ground lay within that ring
To which he only dared to cling ;
Renouncing here, as worse than dead,
The craven few who bowed the head
Beneath the change ; who heard a claim
How loud ! yet lived in peace with shame.

That Wordsworth did not trouble himself over much
with details, is shown by the fact, that he believed the
ruins to be those of a religious house, as witness the
line, " There stood a consecrated pile, where tapers
burned and mass was sung ; " and again, on the
Brownie's death, " How he was found, cold as an
icicle, under an arch of that forlorn abode ; " nevertheless we are grateful to this great English poet in
that he was responsive to the beauty and significance
of the scene ; so many pass that way with no thought
for the " glory that has departed."

FROM " THE SPAEWIFE."

In " The Spaewife," that great romance of the
Lennox, John Galt also has something to interest us.
Appended are extracts :—
" A sedate shelty was accordingly provided to carry
Bishop Finlay over the hills, and the skin of an otter,
or selgh, was laid on its back, as an emblem and substitute for a saddle ; two thongs cut from the hide of a
cow were as stirrups, for in those days tanned leather
was not amongst the Celts ; and for the bridle there
was another thong ; and the bit, which was put into
the mouth of the Bishop's shelty, was the key of the
Provost of Dumbarton's door, which the chief of the
MacFarlanes had, a short time before, taken away with
him, when in the town on a harrying visitation, but

which had been rescued by some of the Earl of Lennox's men, with all the other spoil, as the MacFarlanes were returning home to Arrochar."

―――――

" Surely you have not seized the unfortunate Duchesse (of Lennox) without authority," exclaimed the Earl (of Athol). " Know you not that the king has offered to restore her all the earldom of Lennox, which however "—

" All the earldom—oomph. Sowlls and podies ! Is 't the king a man wi' a sholder on a head ? And will mi Laidie Tooches pe making a lifting pack again o' the cows and the cattle tat te Macfarlane—oomph. Got dam te Macfarlane ; he took te cows and cattle when te king made his judifications—oomph."

" Of course, Glenfruin," said the Earl, " you were too faithful to herry the lands of Lennox at the time of the forfeiture. But if The MacFarlane has done so, let him look to the consequences, unless he has a friend to appease the King."

―――――

" It was agreed between them (Celestine Campbell and his mother, the Lady of Loch Aw) that Celestine, with a numerous train, under the pretext of hunting, should by break of day make towards Lennox whither . . . the Lord James (only surviving son of Murdoch, Duke of Albany and Isabella Countess of Lennox) had often spoke of going to raise, among the friends of his mother's family, the means of bidding adieu to Scotland for ever.

Celestine passed through Glencroe, and reached Loch Long head before he heard any tidings. It was not indeed until he had claimed entertainment from MacFarlane in the castle of Arrochar . . . that he obtained any information to guide his search.

B

It chanced on that night as he was sitting at supper discoursing with MacFarlane of his exploits as a hunter, that he recounted how, in returning from his late excursion beyond Ben Cruachan, he had fallen in with Sir Aulay Macaulay. (Lord James Stuart, at this time, passed under the name of Sir Aulay Macaulay). For The MacFarlane, notwithstanding the insinuations of Glenfruin to the contrary, happened then to be one of the most orderly and loyal of all western chieftains, and on that account Campbell did not choose to tell him, that he had been even so far as Loch Rannochside. Whether there was anything particular in the sound of his voice, or in his look, when he spoke of this adventure, it was certainly not remarked either by MacFarlane himself, nor by any of the kinsmen then seated at the table with them ; but while Campbell was speaking, he was startled by the apparition of two bright and glittering eyes shining in an obscure corner in the hall over against him ; and in a moment after, the voice of the Spaewife was heard chanting from the same place:—

"Sir Aulay Macaulay, the Laird of Cairndhue,
Bailie of Dumbarton, and Provost of the Rhue.' '

" O never mind her ! " said MacFarlane ; " it is that poor wandering creature, Anniple of Dunblane ; she came into the hall a short time before yourself. They say she knows something by common ; but whether it be so or not, she's a harmless thing, and is aye free of a night's lodging here."

" Aye," interposed Anniple, dragging herself forward without rising : " it's well known that I ken something—

"Sir Aulay Macaulay, the Laird of Cairndhue,
Bailie of Dumbarton, and Provost of the Rhue."

" Well," said Campbell, " and what know you of him ? Have you seen him lately ? How was it with him ? "

She, however, made no answer, but sang :—

" This night beneath the greenwood tree
My love has laid him down ;
And the bells will ring, ring merrilie,
Or they wile him to the town."

" Who is your love ? " said Campbell eagerly, struck by something peculiar in her manner.

" Sir Aulay Macaulay, the Laird of Cairndhue,
Bailie of Dumbarton, and Provost of the Rhue."

Campbell perceived that she had some notion of the anxiety with which he had asked the questions ; but afraid of being too curious lest he might attract observation, he smiled to MacFarlane, as if at Anniple's rhapsody, and casting a slight glance towards her, resumed the conversation which she had interrupted.

(Next morning, it may be stated, Anniple met Campbell on his way to Tarbet and led him over the hills to Glen Fruin where he attained his desire of meeting Lord James. Galt need not have feared to have made Campbell take MacFarlane into his confidence, for however well affected towards King James, it is inconceivable that a MacFarlane chief would have betrayed a scion of the house of Lennox, his own kith and kin.—*Editor*).

The danger Lord James ran in Glen Fruin is illustrated by the following remark of the hypothetical chieftain of that name to Campbell during their sojourn at his castle.

" Al in good time, Celestine Campbell, my very goot young friend, and we will pe telling you al. Do you know, King's herald, tat te Macaulay—ah he is te false and te traitor, too—oomph ! was na he wi' te Lord Hameis (James) and tat Peeshop o' Pelzeebub, te Peeshop o' Lismore when tey prunt te town o' Dumbarton—and to MacFarlane—God tam te Mac-Farlane—he lifted al te cattles from te lands o' Lennox,

and te Glenfruins were na left te halph of a two-score—
oomph! And would na it pe a pail and a ransom for
Glenfruin to te King's Majestie—to catch te Macaulay
—oomph!"

A further interesting extract is from a volume,
published at Jena, in 1866, by Dr. Richard Andree,
" Vom Tweed zur Pentlandfohrde." In this account
of a visit to Scotland the author gives a picture of a
splendid specimen of the race :—

" At the gate of Taymouth Castle he was met by an
old keeper. The old MacFarlane was a magnificent
figure of a Highlander. He had eighty years behind
him, yet he was fresh and strong for his age, his gait
was straight and upright, his hair silver-white, his
cheeks rosy. The naked calves, that showed from
under his short Campbell tartan kilt, were rigid as a
young man's, and the years had not been able to
quench the fire of his eyes. They shone with a strange
brilliance when he spoke of his eventful life. In his
early years he had been a soldier, and had served with
Wellington in the Peninsula. Later he fought with
the Forty-Second Highland Regiment at Waterloo.
Later he fought against Napoleon's breast-plated
cavalry. He had seen the nobility of France in flight,
and had turned back home to the mountains of his
beloved Scotland."

In later times Neil Munro in his fine Highland novels,
particularly " Doom Castle," makes frequent references
to the clan, but in its decay. He appears to regard our
progenitors as a race of freebooters without a redeeming
quality, but that was necessary for his purpose.

It would seem that the greater the distance from the
ancient home, the greater becomes the clansman's love
of the old traditions. Many years ago, a Mrs.
Macfarlane Little, of Statin Island, U.S.A., spent a
long holiday at Arrochar, collecting material for a book,
which she subsequently published under the title of
" Clan Farlan."

While guilty of several serious inaccuracies, Mrs. Little is entitled to our acknowledgments for making the first serious effort towards collecting, in permanent form, the history and records of the clan. That she was imbued with the zeal and fervour of the true clanswoman there can be no doubt. That spirit breathes through the impressions of her first visit to Arrochar; written in 1891.

" As we neared Arrochar, the loch, now reaching its head, narrows till it is but half a mile wide. The scenery becomes grand, sublime, awesome. The towering mountains, between which we glide, seem to come down and bathe their feet in the placid waters. Their sides are treeless, green to their summits, with patches of bare brown rocks just visible through the short grass, with here and there a yellow flaming bush of the ' bonny, bonny broom.'

The rain, which had fallen for several days, had sent rills down these steep sides till they foamed like rifts of snow from top to bottom. The hoarse thunder, hurled from peak to peak, added grandeur to the scene, until the sun suddenly burst out, as if to give the wanderers a welcome, and a rainbow lay down the mountain side, its gay colours touching the water.

" The loch, which had been black, in a few minutes reflected the mountains, till one might have fancied it a grassy lawn.

" When the sun dropped like a ball of fire behind the mountains that, grouped, stand like grim sentinels over the little hamlet, they became violet-coloured, then took on the hue that one sees on a great purple plum, with the ' down ' upon it.

" On the western side of the loch rise Ben Ime and Cuilessen Hill, while beyond and above rises, in great majesty and grandeur, Ben Arthur, also called the Cobbler, to a height of 2,400 feet ; his fantastic peak so cracked and broken by countless years of frost and rain that it bears a striking resemblance to a cobbler at work, his wife in front of him, with a ' mutch ' upon her head.   This is one of the range that presents so formidable an appearance, and is pointed out to the tourist descending Loch Lomond as the Arrochar Mountains.

"From the Inn at Arrochar the traveller winds around the head of Loch Long, passing the gates of beautiful Stronafine, crossing the picturesque stone bridge, beneath which the Taing flows into the loch, and skirting the western shore by a road cut from the side of the mountain, turning to the right within a few yards of Ardgarten, and enters Glencroe, a desolate but magnificent glen guarded on the right by Ben Arthur. The steep carriage-road winds up for seven miles; while upon the summit may be found a stone bearing the very appropriate inscription, "Rest and be thankful." Descending upon the other side, some miles away, lies Inveraray Castle, the seat of the Duke of Argyll.   As our traveller retraces his steps and crosses again the bridge, at his left lies Glenloin, up which cattle have often been driven by the light of MacFarlane's ' lantern.'   In the distance Ben Voirlich is seen, upon whose side is the ' lonely tarn,' Loch Sloy. Along the eastern side of the loch are the houses of Arrochar, built all of grey stone, and half concealed by hedges of the green shining hawthorn.   On an eminence overlooking the water, stands ' Arrochar House,' surrounded by its well kept, flower-decked, lawns and noble trees; just below are the Established Church and Manse, the latter a commodious house, its grey walls brightened by the ivy and magnificent climbing roses that attain such perfection in the climate; here, too, are velvet lawns and lofty trees, and wherever the eye turns, it meets a view of sublimity and grandeur; a rare spot in this vale of solitude, a home well suited to the quiet, cultured tastes of its happy and contented inmates.

"On this side some mighty power seems to have

ARROCHAR HOUSE, PRESENT DAY.

Note the three sections. The front part was built by Sir James Colquhoun and the centre by the Duke of Argyll, between 1784 and 1799. The rear portion is part of Inverioch House, built 1697.

said to the eternal mountains, ' Stand back ! ' for from
this point runs the Isthmus that connects Arrochar
and Tarbet—Loch Lomond and Loch Long. The
fine macadamised road, two miles in length, with
hedges in which the birds were singing, and ancient
oaks on either side, was once the broad avenue that ran
through MacFarlane's Park. On the left of this road
leaving Arrochar may be seen a small fragment of stone
foundation, said to have been a stronghold in which
MacFarlane placed his family when the Danes ravaged
Arrochar in 1263.

" Still nearer this last mentioned place, on the right,
the oak trees, which stand with great regularity, here
form a crescent, and the remains of a mound are seen,
said to have been MacFarlane's watch-tower. Just
below the Free Kirk Manse at Tarbet, near the water's
edge, stood the Chief's house, before the old castle was
built at Arrochar, and near it are several mounds.

" A clergyman, whose father was the schoolmaster
at Arrochar, told us that in his boyhood, his companions
would not play there in the gloaming, because, upon
one of these mounds MacFarlane hung his criminals.

" But it is in ' Arrochar House ' our interest centres,
and imagination peoples it with brave men and fair
women. The vision fades, and we now realise that a
century has passed, that this is a new world, the
descendants of our clan are peopling it, and, untram-
meled by the traditions of the past, emancipated from
the gradations of rank, with hand and brain they have
worked out their own destiny, and have heaped wealth,
honour, and distinction upon the ancient and revered
name of MACFARLANE."

But it is not clansmen and clanswomen alone, who
have been impressed by the beauty of the MacFarlane
country. Mr. George Eyre-Todd, a notable student of
Scottish history and folk-lore, has written,

" One of the loveliest regions in the West Highlands
is the district about the head of Loch Long and Loch

Lomond, which was for some five centuries the patrimony of the Chiefs of the MacFarlane clan.   With the
waves of one of the most beautiful sea lochs of the
Clyde rippling far into its recesses, and the tideless
waters of the Queen of Scottish lochs sleeping under the
birch-clad slopes on another side, while high among its
fastnesses, between the towering heights of Ben Arthur
and Ben Voirlich, shimmers in a silver lane the jewel-
like Loch Sloy, this ancient territory could not but, in
the course of centuries, produce a race of men instinct
with the love of the mountains and the moors, and with
all the chivalrous qualities which go to make the
traditional character of the Highlanders of Scotland.
This is nothing less than fact in the case of Clan
Farlan."

Then the Rev. H. S. Winchester, B.D., Minister of
Arrochar, at the time of the Great European War,
expressed similar sentiments :—" The tourist guide-
books and railway time-tables advertise Arrochar as a
peaceful summer resort.   They tell of its lochs and its
fishing streams, of its golf and its pleasant excursions,
its comfortable hotels with their moderate prices.

" Dorothy Wordsworth, looking back upon her sojourn
there, with her brother William, and the poet Coleridge,
remembers Arrochar as a place where it always rains,
where the mountains are grand and the people are
simple, and where every woman carried a green
umbrella.   Burns, who must have been in a specially
bad mood when he passed that way, writes of Arrochar
as ' land of savage hills, swept by savage rains, peopled
by savage sheep, tended by savage people.'

"And the ordinary summer visitor remembers how he
fished in Loch Long, or sweated to the top of the
Cobbler, or tramped the old road up Glen Loin to lonely
Loch Sloy, or crossed Loch Lomond to visit Loch
Katrine and the Trossachs, or sailed to Rowardennan
to climb Ben Lomond.

"Now, however much truth there may be in all these descriptions, none of them tell anything of the really interesting Arrochar, the wild, romantic Arrochar of long ago. And if one were to seek to advertise this romantic Arrochar, he would tell of the grey days when the clouds hang their veils of mystery along the mountain tops, and the mists throw their fringes deep into the valleys; he would speak of the moonlight nights when Loch Lomond lies black and eerie among the shadows, when the Cobbler sees himself reflected from the fairy world which sleeps in the silvery depths of Loch Long, when the owl hoots and the heron screams, and when the ghosts of the wild MacFarlanes look out from the shadow of the rocks, or move noiseless among the black firs on the hill side. He would mention Tighvechtan and Ballyhennan, and Tomua-croich and Tomnahianish, and all the other barbarous-like places which say so little to the stranger but which mean so much. For this is the true Arrochar, the romantic Arrochar, which anyone may see and hear and feel if he will listen to the old folks, and if he will take the trouble to learn the story of the uncouth names.

"Now, if a stranger seeks to interest himself in these matters, the first thing that strikes him is this—wherever he turns he meets the MacFarlanes. If it be the name of the parish—its meaning is found in a MacFarlane charter; the odd-looking place names—they had their origin in some deed of a MacFarlane; the tales of the old folks—the motif of every one is some doing of the MacFarlane; the church records, the church bell, the very chalices for Holy Communion, the mark of the MacFarlane is over them all. One then begins to realise the full meaning of the words in the 'old statistical account' of Arrochar, written about 1790. 'The greater part of the people of this parish are MacFarlanes, who have always had, till lately, a strong attachment to their chief . . . . .'

" Arrochar is now a peaceful summer resort among the hills. Tighnaclach and Tighness sleep by the sparkling waters of Loch Long ; Tarbet nestles in its trees in the sunshine, and looks out on the dark Loch Lomond, stretching in shady bays and wooded headlands far into the shadow of the Ben ; the stronghold on Eilan-a-bhuth is a bracken-covered ruin among the trees, and nothing is left of the ancient home of the MacFarlanes at Inveruglas except a few black firs upon the hill side, sole survivors of the once great forest which covered the land ; and nothing breaks the stillness save the scream of the wild fowl or the sound of the steamer's horn.

"But to one who remembers the Arrochar of other days, there is more in each scene than meets the eye. As evening falls and the mists sweep down the hill sides, he can see the forms of stalwart men, he can catch the gleam of the broadsword, and hear the hoarse shouts of the fray, he can see the driven cattle and the black MacFarlanes out to claim their toll of the Lowland-man's wealth. Or, as the moonlight floods loch and valley and hill tip, till Ben Arthur is seen as clearly in the depths of Loch Long as in the light of midday, the onlooker who remembers, holds his breath lest the wild cry ' Loch Sloy' ring out from Stronafyne hill, and go echoing along Glen Tarbet, to be repeated from hill to hill, till it rouses Portanchuple and Inveruglas, and passes onward to Ardleish and Garabub. Each place name, so grotesque and meaningless, sets loose a phantom procession, stretching back into the mist of the years, the wild picturesque romantic Arrochar of by-gone days."

CHAPTER II.

GILCHRIST.

Earls of Lennox.	Scottish Rulers.
ALWYN, 2nd Earl.	ALEXANDER II., 1214-1239.
MALDUIN, 3rd Earl.	ALEXANDER III., 1249-1286.

GILCHRIST, the founder of the family of Mac-Farlane, was either the fourth or fifth son of Alwyn, second Earl of Lennox.

From his brother, Earl Malduin, he obtained for his patrimony, the lands and barony of Arrochar in the upper part of the earldom of Lennox, as is shown by the following extract from the original charter :—

" Terras de superiori Arrochar de Luss jacentes inter rivulos qui vocantur Aldyvach et Aldquchulin ex una parte, et rivulos qui vocantur Hernan Hinys et Trostan ex altera parte, una cum insulis de Elanvow, Elanvanow Elanrouglas et Elaig."

Translated, this reads—

" The lands of Upper Arrochar down from Luss, lying between the small brooks which are called Aldyvach and Oldquchulin on one side and the small brooks which are called Hernan Hings and Trostan on the other side, together with the islands of Elanvow, Elanvanow, Elanrouglas and Elaig."

This charter bears no date, but was granted in the reign of King Alexander II., between 1225 and 1239, probably in the first mentioned year, upon Malduin becoming Earl of Lennox by the death of his father, Alwyn.

The terms of this charter were subsequently confirmed in a similar document granted to John, the seventh Chief of MacFarlane, on 13th February, 1420, under the Great Seal of King James I. of Scotland.

Gilchrist, under the designation of " Brother of the Earl," appears as witness to many of Earl Malduin's charters granting lands to vassals. Of special interest is one to Anselm MacBeth of Buchanan, of the Isle of Clare-Inch in Loch Lomond, dated in 1225, and another to William, son of Arthur de Galbraith, of the two carrucates of Baldernock, dated at Fintry in 1238.

Haco's devastating foray of 1263 probably occurred in Gilchrist's time. Olaf, King of Man, with sixty ships, appeared in Loch Long. The landing of the Norsemen at the head of the loch was opposed by the Arrochar people who suffered defeat. The battle was fought at Ballyhennan, on some raised ground immediately to the west of the railway embankment and a little below the public road. Above the village of Arrochar, according to tradition, stood a stronghold in which the Chief is said to have placed his family for security. Further along the short valley, lying between Arrochar and Tarbet, is the ancient burial ground of Ballyhennan, a little to the east of the battlefield. Here it is said the clansmen slain in the battle were interred. Two slight mounds in the grounds of Arrochar House are believed to mark the graves of slaughtered Danes.

After laying waste the country bordering Loch Long (at Knockderry is or was a small fort supposed to be of Danish origin), the invaders ran their vessels ashore at the head of the loch. Unshipping their smaller boats, they dragged these through the valley, and launched them on Loch Lomond. This feat is described in the Norwegian chronicle.

" The persevering shielded warriors of the throwers of the whizzing spear drew their boats across the broad isthmus. Our fearless troops, exactors of contributions, with flaming brands, wasted the populous islands in the lake, and the mansions around its winding bays."

Loch Lomond, from its retired situation, writes

Irving, had been deemed little exposed to attack; and on some of the islands were numbers of people who, not anticipating the extraordinary measures which the persevering enterprise of the vikings enabled them to carry into execution, had taken refuge in a retreat which they esteemed perfectly secure.

To their terror and dismay, the flotilla of the Norsemen was upon them before any plan of defence could be adopted. Multitudes of the people were put to the sword, and the country around the lake, then a wealthy and populous district, studded with villages, and fertile in agricultural produce, was reduced in a few days to an arid smoking desert, strewn with the dead bodies of the inhabitants, the smouldering fires of plundered granges, and the blackened ruins of cottages and castles.

From Loch Lomond one of the Norse chiefs, named Allan, the brother of Prince Dugal, at the head of a wild multitude, penetrated into the heart of Dumbartonshire and Stirlingshire with similar excesses.

But scarcely had the Norwegians secured their plunder in their vessels in Loch Long, when the fleet was attacked by a hurricane, which drove the whole of the ships from their moorings, and reduced ten of them to complete wrecks.

The storm raged for three days. During that time the Scottish soldiery dominated the Norwegian fleet from the heights above Loch Long and the Firth of Clyde. Haco was finally defeated at the Battle of Largs.

Alluding to the dragging of the boats from Arrochar to Tarbet, Fraser writes, " At this neck of land it was anciently the practise to drag boats across between Loch Long and Loch Lomond. Hence the Gaelic name, Turnbat, which signifies ' draw the boat.' "

CHAPTER III.

DUNCAN—SECOND CHIEF.
1284-1296.

Earls of Lennox.	*Scottish Rulers.*	
MALCOLM, 4th Earl, 1248-1292.	ALEXANDER III.,	1249-1286.
MALCOLM, 5th Earl, 1292-1333.	MARGARET,	1286-1290.
	INTERREGNUM,	1290-1292.
	JOHN BALLIOL,	1292-1296.
	SIR WM. WALLACE,	1296-1305.

GILCHRIST'S son and successor, DUNCAN, was designated in the charters of his times, "Duncanus filius Gilchrist or M'Gilchrist. From his cousin, Malcolm, Fourth Earl of Lennox, he received a charter of confirmation of the lands of Arrochar, whereby the Earl ratifies and confirms :

"Donationem illam quam Malduinus avus meus fecit Gilchrist fratri suo de terris de Superiori Arrochar de Luss coram his testibus Domino Simoni Flandreuse, Domino Duncano filio Amelick, Domino Henrico de Ventere Ponte et Malcolmo de Drumeth."

This reads :—

"That gift which my uncle Malduin made to his brother Gilchrist of the lands of Upper Arrochar down from Luss, in the presence of these witnesses : Master Simon Flandreuse, Master Duncan, son of Amelick, Master Henry of Ventere Ponte (lit. trans. Belly Bridge) and Malcolm of Drumeth."

This charter, although undated (very usual amongst the older charters), by the names of the witnesses, appears to have been granted before 1284. As in the case of the original one granted to Gilchrist, it was subsequently ratified under the Great Seal of King James I. of Scotland.

Duncan appears as a witness to a charter granted by Malcolm, Earl of Lennox, to Michael M'Kessan, of the lands of Garchell and Ballat. He married Matilda, daughter of the Fourth Earl.

It is stated that, after a gallant defence of the national independence, Duncan with most of the great men of his country, was compelled to submit to Edward I. of England. He was one of the subscribers to the bond of submission, called Ragman's Roll, anno 1296. Therein he is designated, Duncanus filius Gilchrist de Levenax.

Duncan is stated to have died soon after that date.

CHAPTER IV.

MALDUIN—THIRD CHIEF.

1314.

Earls of Lennox.	*Scottish Rulers.*
MALCOLM, 5th Earl, 1292-1333.	Sir WM. WALLACE, 1296-1305.
	ROBERT I., 1306-1329.

DUNCAN was succeeded by his son MALDUIN, who, it is recorded, possessed all his father's lands, and inherited his unflinching patriotism. In the train of Malcolm, 5th Earl of Lennox, Malduin was a faithful adherent of Robert the Bruce, succouring and shielding his king after his memorable escape from the Macdougalls of Lorn at Tyndrum in the winter of 1306.

It was after the battle at Methven, Bruce had taken shelter in Donside, but finding himself in danger even there, he crossed the mountains, meaning to seek refuge in Kintyre. He had just reached Tyndrum, at the entrance to Glenfalloch, when he was waylaid by the Macdougalls, and escaped with the utmost difficulty. Then, by some strange mischance, he and his followers, after descending Glenfalloch, found themselves on the east side of Loch Lomond, whereas the road to Kintyre lay through Tarbet Glen on the western side. Barbour tells the tale of how, when the hunted king and his little company were wandering down the steep and pathless banks, seeking for a means to cross, Douglas at length found an old boat, which, with much patching and mending, could ferry over two men at a time; how, all through the long night, the weary band stood and waited, while the little boat went and came, till all were safely ferried across to the western shore. At Firkin, about three miles south of Tarbet, there stands an ancient yew, still known as Bruce's tree. Under the shelter of this tree, Bruce stood in the midst of his followers who had crossed, entertaining them with tales of chivalry all that night, and wiling away the time, while the frail boat was plying its journeys.

A little way up Glenloin is Bruce's cave, which is large and commodious, and could hold about fifty men. Here, runs the legend, the king and his followers found shelter for the night before commencing their long journey by Glencroe to Argyllshire and the safety of Kintyre.

Bruce's adventures in the Arrochar country are thus detailed by Barbour :—

" While hunting on the hills of Arrochar they were joined by Malcolm, Earl of Lennox, who, under every reverse, remained true to Bruce, and who, to protect himself from the English, had been compelled to seek shelter in the fortresses of his earldom. The Earl had not seen the King since his defeat at Methven, and having learned nothing concerning him, had been apprehensive that, exposed as he was to so many dangers, he had probably gone the way of all the earth. At the very time that Bruce and his companions were engaged in the chase, Lennox happened to be similarly occupied in the neighbourhood. Having heard the sound of the King's hunting horn, he was struck with surprise, and on making inquiries, discovered who the illustrious strangers were, upon which, along with his attendants, he hastened to the spot whence the sound proceeded, and found his beloved sovereign. The joy of the monarch and of his faithful subject, who had not seen each other for a protracted period, at this unexpected meeting may be imagined. Lennox fell upon his royal master's arms, and, big with emotion, burst into tears, while Bruce, not less deeply moved, tenderly clasped his arms around the Earl, and spoke

c

to him in encouraging and hopeful words. All the lords of Bruce's party present, gladdened at meeting with Lennox and his friends, gave demonstration of their warm affection towards them, the more so that friends now met, who not only had not seen each other for many a day, but who were even ignorant of each other's safety. This natural burst of joy, mingled with sadness, having subsided, the Earl did not fail to observe the wretched plight to which his sovereign and his followers were reduced ; and delighted that he had now an opportunity of giving substantial proofs of his loyalty, he quickly conducted them to a secure retreat, where they were provided with an abundant repast, such as they had not for a long time enjoyed. All having partaken heartily of the repast, the King rose up, and, with all the fervour of his heart, thanked the Earl for his noble and generous hospitality, and expressed the joy which this unexpected meeting had, under the circumstances, caused to them all. At the request of Bruce, Lennox and his friends related their perilous adventures and hardships in their efforts to escape capture by the English. This relation touched the chords of sympathy in Bruce's heart, and in his turn he rehearsed the dangers, toils, and troubles, through which he himself had passed since he had last seen them. The tempest-tossed warriors, having thus recounted their respective adventures, behoved now to part ; for Arrochar, though the territories of the Earl of Lennox and his cousins the MacFarlanes, could not at that time have afforded a secure asylum for Bruce. To have prolonged his stay in a district adjoining that of Argyll, where were powerful families, all friends of the Comyns, and all at the service of the Lord of Lorn, who had complete possession of the roads and passes, would have been dangerous, and, besides, many of the Earl's vassals, in the hope of reward, were ready, should opportunity offer, to violate their allegiance by arresting the King and delivering him up to the

English. Accordingly, Bruce having reminded the Earl that time being urgent, he must hasten to Kintyre; and having entreated Lennox to follow speedily, with such a number of men as he could collect in his earldom on the spur of the moment, bade him farewell, and pressed forward to Kintyre.

The magnanimous Earl made haste to join his royal master, but in passing down the Firth of Clyde with his men he was pursued by some galleys manned with a hostile party of the district, from which he escaped only by lightening the galley in which he was conducted, to enable it to sail the faster."

As he had been partner in his adversities, the Chief of MacFarlane was also partaker in the king's subsequent successes. The clan, under the banner of Lennox, was present at the Battle of Bannockburn, and shared in the honour and glory of that great achievement.

Robert I. granted a charter to Dougal MacFarlane of the lands of Kindowie and Argushouche, etc., but who this Dougal was we are unable to discover.

1186804

CHAPTER V.

PARLAN—FOURTH CHIEF.

1329.

Earls of Lennox.	*Scottish Rulers.*
MALCOLM, 5th Earl, 1292-1333.	DAVID II., 1329-1371.
DONALD, 6th Earl, 1333-1373.	

ALL that is known of the son of Malduin is that he lived in the reign of David II., but his place in this chronicle is of first importance, as he gave a permanent surname to his house and his Clan.

The Gaelic Pharlan or Partholan means in English Bartholomew. As we have seen, the second chief was known as Duncan MacGilchrist (son of Gilchrist), and presumably Malduin's surname was MacDuncan or MacGilchrist, but from Pharlan's son onwards the surname MacFarlane became fixed.

There are at least two later instances of a cadet taking his father's Christian name as surname. The sept of MacAllan is descended from the son of an Allan MacFarlane, while the descendants of a chief's son, referred to later, eschewed the clan name and described themselves as Thomsons or Thomasons (sons of Thomas). There are besides, many instances of the rank and file of the Clan taking other names, or of having these bestowed upon them, which accounts for the numerous septs. Some of these changes were due to the clansman's vocation, as Stalker, Miller, etc., but others were adopted from motives of prudence, when the Clan came into conflict with the authorities. MacIan in presenting the family coat-of-arms, previous to the addition of the well known demi-savage crest,

spells the name above the device MacPharlan.   To-day
we have such variants as MacFarlan, MacFarlane,
McFarlane, MacFarlin, and MacFarland, but they are
all " Jock Tamson's bairns.".

Buchanan writes :—" Malduin's son and successor
was Partholan or Parlan, from whose proper name the
family obtained the patronomical name of McPharlane
or Pharlansons, being, as it is asserted, for three
descents before the assumption of this, surnamed
McGilchrist.   Some of these have retained that surname
(McGilchrist) as yet, who nevertheless own themselves to be cadets of the family of MacFarlanes."

Strangely enough, MacGilchrist is not now regarded
as a sept of MacFarlane, being attributed to the
Ogilvys and MacLachlans.

CHAPTER VI.

MALCOLM—FIFTH CHIEF.

1344-73.

Earls of Lennox.	*Scottish Rulers.*
DONALD, 6th Earl, 1333-1373.	DAVID II., 1329-1371.
WALTER, 7th Earl, 1373-1385.	ROBERT II., 1371-1390.

MALCOLM MACFARLANE, so designed in the two following charters, succeeded his father, Parlan or Bartholomew, and obtained from his cousin, Donald, Earl of Lennox, upon the resignation of his father, Bartholomew, son of Malduin, a charter of confirmation of the said lands and islands, in as ample a manner as his predecessors held the same, as the charter itself, yet extant, expressly bears :—

" Adeo libere, quiete, et honorifice, in omnibus et per omnia, sicut charta originalis facta per antecessores nostros, antecessoribus dicti Malcolmi, plenius in se proportat, etc. . . ."

"Testatur, hiis testibus Malcolmo Fleming Comite de Wigton, Joanne Steuart de Dernley, Patricio Fleeming de Weddal, militibus, etc."

" As equally, as freely, amply, peacefully and honourably in ·all points as in the charter granted by our predecessors to the said Malcolm's ancestors, the right devolves on him, etc.—Witnesses, Malcolm of Wigton, John Stewart of Darnley, Patrick Fleming of Weddal (soldiers)."

This charter seems, by the witnesses, to have been granted about the year 1344.

He received also from the said Earl another charter dated Bellach, May 4th, 1354, whereby the Earl freely discharges him and his heirs of four marks of feu duty, payable yearly out of the said lands, and that, "not only for bygones, but even also for the time to come."

Malcolm married, but who the lady was, is not known. By her he had a son, Duncan.

"We must here observe," writes the historian, "that Donald, sixth Earl of Lennox, dying without sons anno 1373, in him ended the whole male line of the three elder sons of Alwyn, second Earl of Lennox, whereby the representation of that noble family devolved upon Malcolm MacFarlane, his undoubted heir male (being grandson's grandson of Gilchrist, fourth son of Earl Alwyn). But as the said Earl, Donald, contrary to the ancient feudal system, left his whole estate to his daughter, Countess Margaret, this Malcolm MacFarlane declined claiming a dignity which he thought he had not estate sufficient to support. He died soon thereafter and was succeeded by his son, Duncan."

CHAPTER VII.

DUNCAN—SIXTH CHIEF.

1395-1406.

Earls of Lennox.	*Scottish Rulers.*
WALTER, 7th Earl, 1373-1385.	ROBERT II., 1371-1390.
DUNCAN, 8th Earl, 1385-1425.	ROBERT III., 1390-1406.
	JAMES I., 1406-1437.

DUNCAN, promiscuously designated "of that Ilk," and of Arrochar, was the son of Malcolm. He received from Duncan, 8th Earl of Lennox, described as his cousin, a charter of confirmation of his lands, which is dated at the Earl's "Mansion-house of Inchmirin," 10th June, 1395. In this charter Duncan is designed "Dilectus et specialis noster Duncanus MacFarlane filius et haeres quoncham Malcomi MacFarlane domini de Arrochar." (Our chosen and special Duncan MacFarlane, son and heir formerly of Malcolm MacFarlane, Lord of Arrochar). The witnesses to this charter are Walter Buchanan of that Ilk, Humphrey Colquhoun, first of that surname to be laird of Luss, Niel of Balnory, Duncan Campbell of Gaunan, and Malcolm McAlpine. The lands, as described in this charter were, "between the river Dynach and Aldanchwhyn on the one side, and the rivers Arnan, Innis and Trostane on the other side, with the islands of Elanvow, Elanvanow, Elan-dowglas and Elaig, in the Earldom of Lennox."

Duncan married Christian Campbell, a daughter of Sir Colin Campbell of Lochow, ancestor of the Dukes of Argyll. This marriage is attested by a liferent

SPECIMEN OF A MACFARLANE CHARTER.

charter granted by Duncan in favour of Christian, of the lands of Keanlochlong, Inveriock, Glenluin and Portcable, before the following witnesses, John Campbell, Dean of Argyle, Duncan Campbell of Gaunan, John McColman, etc. This charter is also dated 1395.

Besides his eldest son, John, who succeeded him, Duncan had another son named Thomas, who founded the family of Clachbuy, cadets of which are dispersed through the Western Isles. From his proper name, Thomas's descendants called themselves MacCauses (Thomas's sons) or Thomson. These are included amongst the septs of the Clan.

Duncan died in the reign of James I.

Another account, by the Rev. A. MacLean Sinclair, LL.D., says Duncan's children were :—Duncan, Colin, David, and a daughter.

CHAPTER VIII.

JOHN—SEVENTH CHIEF.

1426.

Earls of Lennox.	*Scottish Rulers.*
COUNTESS ISABELLA, 1425-1452.	JAMES I., 1406-1437.
	JAMES II., 1437-1460.

JOHN, son of Duncan, married Jean, daughter of Sir Adam Mure, of Rowallan, and sister of Elizabeth Mure, first wife of King Robert II., and is witness to a charter granted in the year 1426. He died in the beginning of the reign of James II.

That practically nothing is chronicled relating to this chief, may be due to the fact that the adherents of Lennox and Albany were, like their lords, under the king's displeasure.   Duncan, the aged Earl of Lennox, and Murdoch, Duke of Albany, his son-in-law, husband to the Countess Isabel, with two of their sons were all executed in 1425.

We have noted that the charters of Gilchrist and his son Duncan were confirmed under the Great Seal of James I. in 1420, but as that date is prior by four years to the beginning of the king's actual reign, on his return from exile in England, the presumption is that these confirmations were the act of Albany as Regent, on representations made by the Chief of MacFarlane through the Earl of Lennox.

CHAPTER IX.

DUNCAN—EIGHTH CHIEF.

1441.

Earls of Lennox.	*Scottish Rulers.*
COUNTESS ISABELLA, 1425-1452.	JAMES II., 1437-1460.
	JAMES III., 1460-1488.

DUNCAN was served, and returned, heir to his father on January 18th, 1441. He had two sons, Walter, his heir, and John, progenitor of the MacFarlanes of Kenmore, from whom are descended the MacFarlanes of Muckroy, Auchinvenal More, and Dunnamaninch in the North of Ireland. Auchinvenal More is in Glen Fruin, and Muckroy in Argyllshire. Kenmore is on Lochlomondside between Tarbet and Inveruglas.

Duncan died in the reign of James III.

The battle of Stalc, fought 1468, belongs either to Duncan's period or that of his son, Walter. A stone commemorating this clan fight was erected by Lt.-Col. A. King Stewart of Acknacor, Appin, and bears this inscription :—

A.D. 1468.

"Above this spot was fought the bloody battle of Stalc, in which many hundreds fell, when the Stewarts and Maclarens, their Allies, in defence of Dugald, Chief of Appin, son of John Stewart, Lord of Lorn and Innermeath, defeated the combined forces of the MacDougalls and MacFarlanes."

The scene of the battle lies just behind the monument —a veritable shell crater, but on a more magnificent scale than the modern ones. Stalc is in Appin, Argyll, and we are inclined to assume that some of the Argyllshire MacFarlanes were the allies of the MacDougalls on this occasion, as Appin is " a far cry " from Arrochar.

CHAPTER X.

WALTER—NINTH CHIEF.
1488.

Earls of Lennox.   *Scottish Rulers.*
INTERREGNUM.   JAMES III., 1460-1488.

IN a charter under the Great Seal, from King James III., to the town of Dumbarton, Walter MacFarlane of that Ilk is designated "Domi de Arrochar," etc.   This charter is dated 1486.

He married the only daughter of James, second Lord Livingstone, and by her had two sons, Andrew, who succeeded him, and Dugal, who founded the family of Tullichintall (Tullich is in and around Glen Douglas), from whom come the MacFarlanes of Finart, Gorton, etc.

If the story of " The Piebald Horse " is to be accepted as fact, Walter ended his career on the field of Sauchieburn, in 1488.

There seems no doubt that following the decay of their parent house of Lennox, the Clan of MacFarlane, either in Walter's time or that of his son, Andrew, passed through a perilous period.   The whole reign of James III. was disturbed by the rebellions of the great barons.   Taking · advantage of the weakness of the king, the heirs general to the lands of Lennox, John Stewart, Master of Darnley, and Sir John Haldane of Gleneagles, descended respectively from the third and second sisters of the Countess Isabella, advanced pretensions also, to the title of *Earl* of Lennox. Darnley, after the death of the Countess Isabella, in 1452, actually assumed the dignity without warrant. Apparently the Chief of MacFarlane revived the claim

of heir male, and, according to the accounts of Brown
and Buchanan, " offered a strenuous opposition to the
pretentions of the feudal heir. Their resistance,
however, proved alike unsuccessful and disastrous.
The chief and all his family perished in defence of what
they believed to be their just rights. The Clan
suffered severely, and of those who survived the
struggle, the greater part took refuge in remote parts
of the country. Stewart of Darnley finally overcame
all opposition and succeeded to the Earldom of Lennox
in 1488.

The destruction of the Clan would now have been
inevitable, but for the opportune support given by a
gentleman of the Clan to the Darnley family. He had
married a daughter of John Stewart, who became
ninth Earl of Lennox, to whom his assistance had been
of great moment at a time of difficulty. He saved the
remnant of the Clan, and recovered the greater part of
their hereditary possessions.

Andrew, however, does not appear to have possessed
any other title to the chiefship than what he derived
from his position, and the circumstance of his being
the only person in a condition to afford them protection ; in fact, the Clan refused him the title of Chief,
which they appear to have considered incommunicable,
except in the right line ; and his son, Sir John
MacFarlane, accordingly, contented himself with
assuming the title of "Captain of the Clan."

We have quoted the passage in full, in order to
contradict the last paragraph. These historians have
manifestly based their assumptions on a belief that
Captain was a title inferior to, or differing from, that of
" Chief," whereas the two are interchangeable terms.
It is inconceivable that there existed a MacFarlane,
other than the chief, with sufficient power—that is to
say, in men—to be of any real service to the Master of
Darnley, and of such station as to command the hand
of his daughter in marriage. We prefer to rely upon

Douglas and Nisbet, who give this " gentleman of the Clan " as the actual son of Walter, the ninth chief. We suggest that the probabilities are, that when the Clan made its submission to Darnley after the defeats above recorded, the compact was cemented by the marriage of the chief with one of Darnley's daughters. Such an arrangement was consonant with Darnley's policy to win to his cause the principal men of the Lennox against his rival Haldane, who, with the exception of MacFarlane the undoubted heir male, had certainly a prior claim, being senior to Darnley as a cadet of the Lennox family.

In 1473 Darnley obtained a royal precept declaring him heir, not only of half the lands, but of the title of Earl of Lennox, and was finally invested in it, as Buchanan states, in 1488.

Now, to reconstruct the situation upon the basis of history. We know that Darnley supported the barons, in whose possession was the prince, afterwards James IV., against James III. If Walter MacFarlane, as seems probable, supported the king, what is more likely than that Darnley, already in possession of the chief Lennox strongholds, Inch Murrin and Catter, in retaliation, carried fire and sword into the Arrochar country ? This theory also lends colour to the probability of the death of Walter in James's crowning catastrophe, Sauchieburn, as suggested by the Piebald Horse Legend. Afterwards Walter's son, Andrew, in the changed conditions brought about by the death of James III., would make peace with Darnley in the manner suggested. The idea that a cadet assumed the chieftaincy appears to have arisen from a later Latin charter in which Sir John MacFarlane was styled " capitaneus de Clan Pharlane." This, Skene, in his " Highlanders of Scotland," took to mean " Captain of Clan Farlane," but Dr. M'Bain, editor of the latest edition of the work, points out that Capitaneus is really Latin for Chief.

Legend of "The Piebald Horse."

The following is the legend of " The Piebald Horse," as set down by the Rev. James Dewar, Minister of Arrochar.

" In the reign of James III. of Scotland, the Laird of MacFarlane was slain at the battle of Sauchie-Burn, near Stirling, in the year 1488, leaving a widow, who was an Englishwoman, the mother of one son ; he also left a son by his first wife, who was the heir ; but this son and heir had the misfortune to be proud, vain, silly, and a little weak-minded. His half-brother was possessed of a beautiful piebald horse, which had been given to him by some of his mother's relations. The elder brother was about to set out for Stirling and was very desirous of riding this horse, wishing, as the young chief, to make a very grand appearance.

"The step-mother refused the loan of the animal, alleging, as her reason for so doing, her fear that it would not be safely brought back. Her denial only made the young man the more persistent. Finally, a written agreement was drawn up, and signed by the heir, in which he promised to forfeit to his half-brother his lands of Arrochar, in case the horse was not safely returned.

"The step-mother bribed the groom in attendance to poison the horse on the second day from home, and the estate accordingly went to the younger brother.

The Clan refused to receive the latter as their chief, but combined to acknowledge the elder brother as such, though not possessed of the lands of Arrochar. Some years later, by special Act of Parliament, these lands were restored to the rightful heir.

"A ruined gable end on Tullich Hill, above Arrochar, was said to have been the home of the dispossessed heir.

"Another account states that the stepmother caused the stuffing of the saddle to be saturated with poison, which being absorbed by the horse, proved fatal to it.

"In the Lennox, certain MacFarlanes for long were referred to as 'Sliochd-an-eich-bhain,' 'The followers of the piebald horse,' or 'The race of the pyat horse that never was wise,' in contradistinction to Clann-an-Oighre, 'The followers of the heir.' The names MacNuyer, MacNair and MacNeur are said to have had their origin in Clann an Oighre. Walter MacFarlane, 20th chief, the famous antiquary says, MacNair means 'illegitimate,' but we construe this in the sense of 'pretender' to the chieftainship."

CHAPTER XI.

ANDREW—TENTH CHIEF.
1488-1493.

Earls of Lennox.	*Scottish Rulers.*
JOHN (Stewart of Darnley), 9th Earl, 1488-1494.	JAMES IV., 1488-1513.

AS stated in the last chapter, Andrew married a daughter of John Stewart of Darnley, afterwards 9th Earl of Lennox, and it may be noted here that following this event the MacFarlanes were as loyal to their new overlords as they had been faithful to their blood relations, the ancient earls.

Andrew appears as a witness in a charter to the burgh of Dumbarton in 1493.

CHAPTER XII.

Sir John—Eleventh Chief.
——1514.

| *Earls of Lennox.* | *Scottish Rulers.* |
| Matthew, 10th Earl, 1494-1513. | James IV., 1488-1513. |

SIR JOHN MACFARLANE was the son of Andrew, and therefore nephew of his contemporary, Matthew, 10th Earl of Lennox.

The honour of knighthood was bestowed upon him by James IV.

In a charter which he granted to one William MacFarlane of the lands of Garrowstuck, Sir John is designated :—

" Honorabilis, Sir Johannes Macfarlane dominus ejusd miles capitaneus de Clan Pharlane, filius Andreae, etc," which is :—

" The honourable Sir John MacFarlane, lord of the same, soldier, captain of Clan Pharlane, son of Andrew, etc."

This charter is the occasion of the misconception, already dealt with, in respect to Sir John being merely " Captain of the Clan," and not Chief. Matthew, the earl, and Sir John married sisters, daughters of James, Lord Hamilton, and nieces of James III. By his wife, whose name is not given, Sir John had two sons, Andrew, his heir, and Robert, who founded the branch of " Inversnait." Sir John married a second time, a daughter of Herbert, Lord Herries, by whom he had a son, Walter of Ardleish. Walter was the progenitor of the MacFarlanes of Gartartan and Ballaggan. Thirdly, Sir John married Lady Helen Stewart,

D

daughter of John, third Earl of Athole, by whom he had a son, John, and a daughter, Grizel.

" Sir John," says the chronicler, " was a man of spirit and resolution, and accompanied King James IV. to the fatal field of Flodden, 1514, where he lost his life fighting gallantly for king and country."

John evidently had a fifth son, named Duncan, In 1545, at Irvine, there was a bond of Manrent (feudal service), entered into by " Duncan, uncle to the laird of MacFarlane " to Hugh MacMaster of Eglinton. At this date Duncan, the son of Andrew, Sir John's grandson, was laird of Arrochar. The first mentioned Duncan was, therefore, a brother of Andrew, the 12th Chief, and a younger son of Sir John. This is confirmed in a Colquhoun complaint of 21st December, 1544, against Duncan MacFarlane of Arrochar, Andrew MacFarlane, Robert MacFarlane and Duncan Mac-Farlane, his fader, brether, *i.e.*, his father and father's brothers.

CHAPTER XIII.

ANDREW—TWELFTH CHIEF.

1514-1544.

Earls of Lennox.	*Scottish Rulers.*
JOHN, 11th Earl, 1513-1526.	JAMES V., 1513-1542.
MATTHEW, 12th Earl, 1526-1571.	MARY, 1542-1567.

ANDREW, known as "Andrew the Wizard," succeeded his father, Sir John. He gained his soubriquet on account of certain tricks of legerdemain, acquired in his travels abroad with one of the MacDonnells of Keppoch. In the records of the Keppoch family there is an autograph letter of a Miss Josephine MacDonnell, written from London, in which "one of the MacFarlanes of Luss" is frequently mentioned as being the friend and college companion of one of the Chiefs of Keppoch, known as Alastair-nan-cleas. They were educated together at Rome, and learned many sleight of hand tricks, with which they astonished and frightened the country people, who ascribed these things to witchcraft. One of Keppoch's daughters married a MacFarlane of Luss, who lived at the time of the above Alastair-nan-cleas.

Andrew frequented the Court of James V. at Holyrood, and married Lady Margaret Cunningham, who was a daughter, either of William, Earl of Glencairn, Lord High Treasurer of Scotland, or Cuthbert, third Earl of Glencairn—the authorities differ. They had two sons, Duncan, his successor, and George of Merkinch. From George are descended the MacFarlans of Kirkton in the parish of Campsie, Stirlingshire, now known as

the Ballancleroch branch.   George settled in the north,
where his posterity continued to reside, until they
bought the lands of Kirkton, when they returned to
be near their kinsmen.

In the biography of Sir Walter Scott is mentioned a
John MacFarlane of this family, who was a friend and
companion of the great Shenachie of the Highlands.

" Andrew, the Wizard," died in the beginning of the
reign of Queen Mary, about 1544, and was an active
supporter of the Regent Lennox during the Queen's
childhood.

The Privy Seal Register of January 30th, 1527,
contains the echo of a Buchanan raid upon the Mac-
Farlanes.   This is a " Respitt " to Patrick Buchanan
and twelve others, mostly of the same name, for
" their treasonable art, part, and assistance, given by
them to George and Robert Buchanan and others,
their accomplices, for the treasonable raising of fire in
the lands of Arrochar, pertaining to MacFarlane ; and
for the cruel slaughter of John Laurenceson and certain
others, being with him in his company, and for the reiff,
spoiling, and harrying of the said town of Fowghe, that
same time ; for XIX. years."

As we have indicated, the MacFarlane chiefs became
zealous supporters of the Lennox Earls.   It was
probably in this character that, shortly after Flodden,
the Clan attacked the castle of Boturick, on the south
shore of Loch Lomond, which was part of the ancient
property of the earldom that had fallen to the share of
Haldane of Gleneagles.   The incident is narrated in Sir
David Lindsay's well known poem, " Squyer Meldrum."
The laird of Gleneagles had fallen at Flodden, and the
Squyer was making love to his widow in Strathearn,
when news came that her castle of Boturick was being
attacked by the MacFarlanes.   Forthwith the valiant
Squyer brought his forces together and rode to the
rescue, driving off the attackers, and securing the fair
lady's property.

Thogail nam bò theid sinn.

Andrew, " the Wizard," is the reputed composer of the famous clan Pibroch, " Thogail nam Bo."

In 1518 Sir John Colquhoun of Luss, his son, Walter, and his brother, Walter, were witnesses to a protest of a person named MacFarlane.

A curious incident is related in Pitcairn's Criminal Trials, under date 16th August, 1536:—" Walter MacFarlane (who may have been Walter of Ardleish, third son of Sir John, the 11th chief, and brother to Andrew, the Wizard), found John Napier of Kilmahew, and John Buntyn of Ardoch, as cautioners for his entry at the next Justice-aire of Dumbarton, to underly the law for art and part of convocation of the lieges in great numbers, in warlike manner, and besetting the way of Margaret Cunningham, widow (second wife) of the late Sir John Colquhoun of Luss, and David Farneley of Colmistoune, being for the time in her company, for their slaughter and for other crimes."

How this matter ended is not known, as the records of the proceedings of Dumbarton Justice-aires at that period have not been preserved. We are, however, relieved to know that Lady Colquhoun was not amongst the slaughtered, for she lived to marry again.

MacLeod, in his History of Dumbarton, tells us something of Andrew's powers in the capacity of Wizard:—

" The chief of the Clan Farlane, when occasion called for it, could use his supposed satanic powers with effect. From his position by inheritance, marriage, and personal properties, he was often at court attending upon the king, and while riding homewards, after one of these visits to Linlithgow, he passed Muillionn Pharaig (Patrick Mill). It was a hot harvest day when he did so, and the miller and his men and maidens were busy reaping a field by the wayside convenient to, and east of, the mill. The chief courteously accosted the miller, and asked a drink for himself and his horse, which the grinder of oats rudely refused. Parched with thirst, very weary, and in no amiable mood, the MacFarlane continued his journey westward, and no sooner had he passed the mill, on which he cast a spell, than its machinery got into motion, seemingly of its own accord. The sound of the grinding caught the miller's ear, and he ordered one of his female reapers to go and stop it. She obeyed so far, but no sooner had she crossed the threshold of the mill than she kilted up her petticoats and set to the dancing, shouting all the while, 'Sud e, suas e! dh'iarr Macpharlain deoch 's cha d'fhuair se e!' 'Up with the dance! MacFarlane sought a drink and did not get it!' A second, a third, and other reaper maidens were sent with like result, and the miller, who ultimately put in an appearance at the mill, beheld with consternation quite a host of kilted females, dancing as if they were mad, and shouting lustily, 'Sud e, suas e! dh'iarr Macpharlain deoch 's cha d'fhuair se e!' The frightened miller sent a man in hot haste after MacFarlane to implore him to return, have his refreshments, and remove the spell he had cast upon the reapers, but he resolutely refused. However, he said to the messenger, 'Go, tell the inhospitable miller to search in the thatch above the mill door, and he will find there a rowan switch, which he is to throw into the mill lade, and that being done, the spell will be removed, and the women will give up their dancing and shouting, and return to their work.'

"These instructions being obeyed to the letter, the women folk were speedily disenchanted, and slowly returned to their labours in the field. Such is the story—partly historical, partly legendary—which has been handed down to our day; and many others of a like nature, relating to the wizard chief, might be added thereto, but space forbids."

CHAPTER XIV.

DUNCAN—THIRTEENTH CHIEF.

1544-1547.

Earls of Lennox.	*Scottish Rulers.*
MATTHEW, 12th Earl, 1526-1571.	MARY, 1542-1567.

DUNCAN, son of Andrew "the Wizard," was a gallant warrior, and took his full share in the martial events of his times. By reason of his near kinship both to Lennox and Glencairn, he frequently assisted them, even to the endangering of his life and fortune.

When Lennox, the father of Henry Darnley, the husband of Mary, Queen of Scots, took up arms in 1544 to oppose the Regent Arran and the catholic party, Duncan, with three hundred men of his surname, joined his forces, and was present at, for them, the disastrous fight of the Butts of Glasgow Muir. Duncan suffered forfeiture, but, by the intercession of his friends, was afterwards restored, and obtained a remission under the Privy Seal. It is stated that a missive was addressed to Lord Ogilvie, Warden of the West, authorising him to allow Duncan MacFarlane of that Ilk to be put in " fre-ward," as he thought expedient, provided the said Duncan found caution to the amount of £1,000 Scots. The Books of Adjournal bear that the caution was forthcoming two days afterwards ; the cautioners being Sir John Campbell of Lundy, Sir John Campbell of Calder, John Campbell of Glen Farquhar, Colin Campbell of Ardkynglass, James Campbell of Lawaries, Archibald Campbell of Glen Lyon, and Arthur Campbell of Ardgarthnay.

The loss of the battle of Glasgow Muir compelled Lennox to withdraw into England, where, having married Lady Margaret Douglas, daughter of the widow of James V. and the Earl of Angus, and so niece of Henry VIII., the Earl secured an English force to assist him, and marched north to resume his campaign.

Although not daring to appear in person after his recent forfeiture and acquittal, Duncan was, nevertheless, wholeheartedly in the Earl's cause, and sent to his aid a hundred and forty well armed men under the command of his uncle, Walter MacFarlane, variously styled as of Tarbet and Ardleish. This detachment of the Clan proved themselves very serviceable in that expedition in the capacity of light troops to the main army. They took part in the taking of the islands of Bute and Arran, the burning of the castles of Rothesay and Dunoon, and in the defeat of the Earl of Argyle.

Writing of these exploits, Ralph Hollinshed in his History of Scotland, says :—" The Earl had with him Walter MacFarlane of Tarbet and seven score men of the head of Lennox that spoke both ' Irishe ' (Gaelic) and the English-Scottish tongues ; light footmen, well armed in shirts of mail and two-handed swords, which, being joined with the English archers and ' shotte,' did much available service in the ' streyghts, marishes, and mountayne countries.' "

In an attempt in August to capture the Castle of Dumbarton, however, Lennox and Glencairn were again defeated.

A warrant of similar indulgence to that of his chief, was however granted to Walter MacFarlane, but on condition of his finding sureties to an amount, this time, of £3,000 Scots. Fortunately cautioners were forthcoming as in the former case, in Andrew, Lord Evandale, Henry, Lord Methven, and Sir John Hamilton of Finnart.

Undeterred by these defeats **and** the consequent

penalties, four months later, in December of 1544, we
find Duncan again on the warpath, despoiling his
immediate Roman Catholic enemies in Dumbartonshire. The far-reaching extent of this invasion, and
the alarm it caused to the authorities, is plainly revealed
in a complaint and representation made to the
Government by the Laird of Luss, contained in letters
issued under the signet of Queen Mary, and dated
21st December, 1544.

" That Duncan MacFarlane of Arrochar, Andrew
MacFarlane, Robert MacFarlane, and Duncan Mac-
Farlane, his fader, brether (father and father's brothers),
Ewer Campbell of Strachur, James Stewart, son to
Walter Stewart in Balquidder, and certain others,
great thieves, limmers, robbers, common sorners upon
our lieges, throatcutters, murderers, slayers of men,
women, and children (the usual general indictment),
and their accomplices, to the number of six hundred
men, and more, came to the said John's lands and place
of Rossdhu, and lands and barony of Luss, and there
cruelly slew and murdered nine of his poor tenants in
their beds, and harried his whole country, both himself
and his poor men, as well as all in sight, goods within
house, as of black cattle, sheep, and other beasts, late
in the month of December, and daily pursued in plain
reiff and sorning upon the poor lieges of our realm, and
are gathered to them many thieves and limmers
intending to harry the whole country. to Glasgow and
Stirling, if they be not resisted, in high contempt of
our authority and law."

These letters, under the signet, were addressed to the
Sheriffs of Argyll, Dumbarton, Renfrew and Stirling,
commanding them to summon all the lieges in these
shires to muster and unite with John Colquhoun of
Luss, and others who might assist him in resisting,
apprehending, and bringing to punishment, the perpetrators of these outrages. After narrating the facts
already stated, the letters proceed :—" Our will is

therefore, and we charge you straitly and command that, incontinently, these our letters pass to the market crosses of our burghs of the said shires, and other places needful, and that there be open proclamation, command, and charge, to all and sundry of our lieges within the bounds of our said sheriffdoms, to rise and come together, for resisting of the said thieves and robbers, to such parties as they shall happen to come upon, and that they take active part with the said John, or any other gentleman that rises for resisting of the said thieves and limmers, and take and apprehend them, and bring them to our justice to be punished for their demerits in conformity with our law." Her Majesty's letters further provided that, should any of the said thieves be slain in the attempt to apprehend them, no crime would attach to the parties killing them, and that all persons, who should fail to obey the proclamation, would be held as taking part with the said thieves and robbers, and would be punished accordingly.

All this ado, although whole counties were summoned to resist the MacFarlanes, apparently resulted in nothing. As a matter of fact, the power of the Crown was at that time very feeble. By the combination of feudal lairds and their vassals, the administration of justice was greatly obstructed, and often rendered impossible.

Duncan was a staunch supporter of the Reformation. Indeed, the ancient chronicler, Buchanan of Auchmar, tells that Duncan Macfarlane of Arrochar was the " first man of any importance in Scotland to make an open profession of the Christian religion "—meaning, of course, the reformed faith.

Although Chief of the Clan for a matter of only three years, his period was one of constant warlike activity. In 1547, about five months before his gallant death, Duncan and fifty-eight of his people were summoned to the justiciary court at Dumbarton, to answer a charge of attacking Sir Patrick Maxwell in his house at

Newark, and of carrying away 280 cattle, 80 sheep, 24 goats, 20 horses, 80 stones of cheese, 40 bolls of barley, and some articles of household furniture.

There is no record to show that the Chief ever appeared to answer the charge, but his son and heir, Andrew MacFarlane, would seem to have made restitution by marrying Sir Patrick Maxwell's daughter; and thus, comments the Rev. H. S. Winchester, the whole affair resolved itself into a rather rough and ready taking of the marriage portion beforehand.

As was seen in the last chapter, Walter of Ardleish had his own grievances against the Colquhouns, for in the previous year, in the month of February, Robert Dennistoun of Colgrain, Walter MacFarlane of Ardleish, Andrew MacFarlane his son and apparent heir, and others, their accomplices, carried away from the Nether and Middle Mains of Luss, sixteen cows which belonged to Sir John Colquhoun of Luss, the price of each being seven merks. Clearly Colquhoun did not recover his " kye," for on 13th February, 1550, or seven years later, and three years after Walter's death, the aggrieved party obtained letters of diligence under the signet of Queen Mary in a process of spulzie, against the depredators, requiring them to appear before the Lords of Council at Edinburgh, on the 16th of March following, to answer for the wrongous, violent, and masterful spoliation by themselves, their servants and accomplices in their names, and the away-taking from the Nether and Middle Mains of Luss, " sixteen tydie kye," the property of Sir John, which they refused to restore, or to give him the value in money."

Duncan met a soldier's death. He, Walter of Ardleish, and a great number of the Clan, gave their lives for Scotland on the Black Saturday of Pinkie, 10th September, 1547. On this, their final stage, these two turbulent spirits fought for Queen Mary.

Duncan was twice married, and both marriages took

place during his father's lifetime. His first wife, Isabel Stewart, daughter of Andrew, Lord Ochiltree, died childless. He afterwards married Catherine Anne Colquhoun, fourth daughter of Sir John Colquhoun of Luss (11th Chief) and Margaret Stewart, who was a daughter of Sir John Stewart, the first Darnley Earl of Lennox. The bridegroom was thus a great-great-grandson and the bride a grand-daughter of the powerful Darnley. The marriage took place, not, as might be supposed, during the lifetime of her father, nor yet during the reign at Rossdhu of Humphrey, her eldest brother, but in the time of her nephew, Sir John Colquhoun, who was Chief of that Clan from 1538 to 1574. On 17th July, 1543, Duncan MacFarlane and Catherine Colquhoun, his spouse, were invested in liferent in the lands of Arrochar, which heritably belonged to Andrew (Duncan's father) and which he had resigned into the hands of Matthew, Earl of Lennox, the superior, for new investment. The original instrument of Sasine is preserved at Rossdhu, and details the lands as follows :—" Jarbolze, Ardlewe, Jarrowstuk, Stukindryne, Ardmurlik, Portcapill, Inner-quhilling, Blairrannyth, and Stronfyne, extending annually to ten pounds of lands of old extent in the earldom of Lennox and shire of Dumbarton. The witnesses were Robert MacFarlane, Patrick Mac-Farlane, John MacFarlane Robertson, Donald Macneill, Thomas Macneill, Dowgall Mackcowll, John M'Kynne, Murdoch Makcalpene, and Sir James Lang, Chaplain, and others."

Duncan and Catherine had two sons, Andrew and Duncan, As his father was killed in 1547, the elder could only have been some three years of age when he succeeded to the headship of the Clan, and twenty-four when he took part in the battle of Langside. Reference to the younger son, Duncan, will be found in the next chapter in regard to the Mill of Nab affair, in 1578.

CHAPTER XV.

ANDREW—FOURTEENTH CHIEF.
1547-1612.

Earls of Lennox.
MATTHEW, 12th Earl, 1526-1571.
HENRY DARNLEY (King Consort
    of Scotland), 1545-1567.
ROBERT, 14th Earl, 1571——.
CHARLES, 15th Earl, —— 1579.

Dukes of Lennox.
ESME, 1st Duke, 1581-1583.
LUDOVIC, 2nd Duke, 1583-1624.

Scottish Rulers.
MARY, 1542-1567.
JAMES VI., 1567-1625.

ANDREW became chief as we have shown in 1547, at the very early age of three years. The first record we have of his activities is in 1560, when he was 16. On 20th July of that year he was witness to a procuratory, dated 20th July, 1560, by Sir Humphrey Colquhoun, rector or prebendary of Kilpatrick-Juxta, in the diocese of Glasgow, for resigning in his name all the rights and fruits of the said rectory into the hands of the most reverend father in Christ, Lord James, Archbishop of Glasgow, or his vicar-general, having power to that effect, as into the hands of the true and undoubted patron, in favour of Sir James Lang, chaplain of the diocese of Glasgow.

In a writ dated 156—, he became a cautioner for Sir John Colquhoun of Luss, for such sums of money as the Lords of Session should modify to be paid to his Majesty and to Humphrey Cunningham, in case the said John should not be able to disprove a pretended obligation produced, or to be produced, by the said

Humphrey against the said John, alleged to be made by his " grandschir."

Next Andrew appears as a magistrate.

On 18th March, 1564, ten individuals, Houston by name, mostly Dumbarton men, were tried in Edinburgh, and, (with one exception), found guilty of " unlawfully convening the lieges," and also of intending to slaughter Andrew Hamilton of Cochno. " It is not improbable," says Irving, " that the attack was made under colour of law, as Hamilton was an adherent of Queen Mary, and with his son, John, was amongst those outlawed after the battle of Langside." The " Assize " on the Houstons included Andrew MacFarlane of Arrochar, with other Lennox notables, John Colquhoun of Luss, Robert Colquhoun of Camstradden, William Smollett, burgess of Dumbarton, and Walter Buchanan of Drumakill.

The chief was now twenty years of age.

Before or about this date Andrew married. His wife was Agnes, daughter of Sir Patrick Maxwell of Newark, by whom he had three sons and one daughter, John, who succeeded him, George, who received for his patrimony the Mains of Kilmaronock (the castle still stands), but left no succession, Humphrey of Brackearn, and Elizabeth, who married Malcolm MacFarlane of Gartartan.

Apparently Andrew had another daughter, as " Duncan of Lochaber " seventeenth (according to Douglas) chief of McGregor, married for his second wife a daughter of MacFarlane of that Ilk. The second son of that lady, Robert, was old enough to be in command of a division at the battle of Glen Fruin in 1603, so his mother must have been born forty years before, which would make her birth year 1563 or earlier. Her father would then be eighteen to twenty, and this rather suggests that she was Andrew's eldest child. This Robert McGregor was a worthy son of his warlike grandfather. He is stated to have been a man of rare martial genius. He laid the plan of attacking the Colquhouns at the famous battle of Glen Fruin, and was given command of a division. To his gallant conduct the success of the day is chiefly attributed, and his sword was long honourably preserved.

BATTLE OF LANGSIDE.

As bold, active, and adventurous as his sire, write the historians, Andrew engaged in the civil wars of the period. A zealous promoter of the Reformation, he was one of the first in the Highlands, of any note, to make open profession of the Protestant religion, and he " went into all the measures of the Earl of Moray against Queen Mary."

The majority of historians are agreed that it was owing chiefly to the assistance given by the Mac-Farlanes that Moray succeeded in defeating the Queen's forces at the battle of Langside, 13th May, 1568. If no great personal advantage accrued therefrom, Andrew, at least, wrote his name indelibly upon the pages of history.

According to a contemporary writer, the battle commenced at nine o'clock in the morning. The Queen's vanguard charged along the Bus-an-'aik (bush and oak) Road to that part of the field where Queen's Park Public School is now situated, and up the existing Lang Loan to the village. There they encountered the Regent's spearmen, while his Hag-butters poured a steady fire on the advancing enemy. The fight which ensued was characteristic of the period. The Regent's left wing was brought up, and by a flank movement charged the Queen's van-guard, striking the men in their "flankes and faces," and forcing them to turn back after long fighting, and pushing and swaying to and fro, as they were locked together in the deadly struggle. " God and the Queen" resounded from one party; " God and the King " thundered from the other. The fresh

attack confused the column of the assailants, and
the dark, dense, and united line of helmets was
broken, and hurled in disorder back upon Clincart
Hill. In vain did the leaders call upon their followers.
They were slain, felled to the earth, and hurried
backwards by the mingled tide of flight and pursuit.
A wild debacle ensued as the now demoralised Queen's
troops were swept down the slopes. From first to
last the battle only lasted three-quarters of an hour.
Yet in that brief time three hundred men were
slaughtered!

Hollinshed's account of the affair reads :—

" In this battle the valiance of a Highland gentleman named MacFarlane stood the Regent's part in
great stead, for in the hottest brunt of the fight he
came in with three hundred of his friends and
countrymen, and so manfully gave in upon the Queen's
people that he was a great cause of disordering them.
This MacFarlane had been lately before condemned to
die for some outrage by him committed, and obtaining
pardon through the suite of the Countess of Moray,
he recompensed that clemency by this piece of service
now at this battle."

Nisbet's account enlarges Hollinshed's :—

" In defence of which (his religion) he (Andrew)
made several signal appearances, particularly at the
famous battle of Langside, fought on May 10th, 1568,
at which battle the Earl of Murray, who was then
Regent, being almost overpowered by the number of
Queen Mary's forces, and his army ready to give way,
the Laird of MacFarlane came in very seasonably to his
assistance with a considerable supply of three hundred
men, with whom he attacked the right wing of the
Queen's army so furiously that they were immediately
obliged to quit their ground, and betake themselves to
their heels, and were soon followed by the rest of the
army. . . . . . He took at the battle three of Queen
Mary's standards which were for a long time preserved

EILEAN-A-VOW CASTLE. BUILT 1577.

in the family. (Also said to have been in Glasgow Cathedral.—*Ed.*). Neither was the Regent insensible of the service the Laird of MacFarlane did him at the battle; for, amongst other rewards, he gave him that honourable crest and motto, which is still enjoyed by his posterity and recorded in the Lyon Register, viz, a demi-savage, proper, holding in his dexter hand a sheaf of arrows, and pointing with his sinister to an imperial crown, or; motto: 'This I'll Defend'; and ever since that time the family have been in use to carry for supporters as above; as is to be seen on the castle of Island Vow, built in the year 1577, by the said Andrew."

The battle is thus described by Sir Walter Scott:—

" They met with equal courage, and encountered with levelled lances, striving like contending bulls, which should bear the other down. The spears of the front ranks were so fastened into each other's armour that the staves crossed like a sort of grating on which lay daggers, pistols and other weapons, used as missiles, which the contending parties had thrown at each other.

" While they were thus locked in an embrace of steel with the Queen's archers pouring a deadly fire into the Regent's men, Andrew MacFarlane threw himself into the fray (with, according to Petrie's Church History, *five* hundred of his own name and dependents) flanking, galling and finally putting the archers to flight."

Browne and M'Ian state that " The MacFarlanes were acknowledged by all to be the chief instrument of obtaining that glorious victory "; and also that the Clan captured three of Queen Mary's standards, " which were long preserved in the family."

Robert MacFarlane of Brooklyn, New York, writing in the Scottish American Journal, under date, February 9th, 1878, states that, " A street in old Rutherglen called the Lennox Road is the path which the

E

MacFarlanes took to cut off the fugitives of Queen Mary's army." As we have said, most of the historians are agreed that the MacFarlanes performed a signal service on this occasion, but that we may not be accused of partiality, we give the following quotation from a volume edited by Mr. Ludovic Mann, issued in Glasgow, in 1918 :—

" A chief of the MacFarlanes, who, scarcely twenty days before the battle, had been condemned to die, had been pardoned by the Countess of Moray. As already indicated, he gathered about 200 of his countrymen, and joined the Regent's army, being attached, apparently, to the east battalion of the Regent's right wing. But during the prolonged tug-of-war there the MacFarlanes wavered. Lord Lindsay, who stood nearest to them, exclaimed that he could fill their places better, and they might go. The freebooting Highlanders, however, rallied when they saw that the Regent's side was winning, returned to the field, pursued the Queen's men, and executed much slaughter."

Why Mr. Mann selected this passage and ignored all the records to the credit of the Clan is between him and his sense of right.

It has been regarded as remarkable that the MacFarlanes should have been found ranged under the banner of the Earl of Moray, when almost all the Highland chiefs espoused the cause of the unfortunate Mary, but as we have seen, Andrew was a zealous Protestant. In those times this would have been a sufficient cause, but he was also bound by ties of loyalty to Lennox, whose heir, Henry Darnley, the king consort, had been foully murdered, as many believed, by Mary's connivance, or at least her passive acquiescence. Even as regards his natural allegiance to the House of Stewart, had the matter rested on that alone, the chief might well have been in a difficulty. His choice lay between the son (albeit illegitimate),

James Stewart, Earl of Moray (and with him the heir to the throne, the future James VI.), and the daughter (already deposed) of James V. A condition of civil war prevailed, and, in such circumstances, a man had to follow his conscience.

We have seen that in 1577, Andrew built the castle on Eilean-a-vow, the ruins of which still stand, and it was doubtless in connection with this event, and in acknowledgment of the services the chief had rendered him, that James VI. paid his recorded visit to the MacFarlane country.

This island was the home of a brood of wild geese, which were supposed to have some mysterious connection with the family, and which, it is said, were never seen again after the ruin of the house.

On the occasion of his visit to the island castle, James, previous to his repast, had been much amused by the gambols of the geese on Loch Lomond. But when one which was brought to the table was found to be tough and ill-fed, James jocularly observed: "that Mac-Farlane's geese liked their play better than their meat"; a proverb which was long current.

In 1578, from the Privy Council Register it would appear that the Clan was guilty of considerable bloodshed, as witness the following, dated Stirling Castle, 26th December, 1578, complaint by Patrick, Lord Drummond, against the Earl of Montrose :—

"Upon the 21st day of December, John, Earl of Montrose, with his servants and accomplices, to the number of forty persons or thereby, in warlike manner, came, under silence of night, to the dwelling house of Wm. Drummond at the Mill of Nab, and surrounded the same for the apprehension of Duncan MacFarlane, brother-german to Andrew MacFarlane of Arrochar, and Duncan MacCoull MacFarlane in Drummond of Lennox, the said Patrick, Lord Drummond's servants being lying in their beds within the said house; for putting of his devised purpose into execution, entered within the said house, and put violent hands upon the persons aforesaid, took them out of their beds, and perforce has transported them to his place of Kincardine; where he as yet detains them as captives and prisoners."

Both parties now appearing personally, and the Earl of Montrose having alleged and produced in his justification a commission, dated 2nd December, given him by the King, "for taking of the said Duncan M'Coull MacFarlane and others, his accomplices, committers of the cruel murder of the late ——— Ra, like as he by vertew thereof took and apprehended him and the said umquhile Duncan MacFarlane, the Lords do two things. They ordain that the Earl of Montrose shall, under pain of horning, ' exhibit the aforesaid persons before them upon the 29th December,' then to hear the cause decided ; but, at the same time, they acquit him from all pain and danger for what he has already done in the matter."

The continuation of the narrative is found under date, Stirling Castle, 29th December, 1578 :—

" The Earl of Montrose, now appearing and presenting his two prisoners, according to the order recorded above, argued that one of them, Duncan MacCoull MacFarlane, having been 'taken by virtue of our Sovereign Lord's commission, for art and part of the cruel murder of the late ——— Ra,' ought not to be set at liberty till he is tried. Lord Drummond, as patron of the prisoners, contended, on the other hand, that the said Duncan MacCoull MacFarlane ought to be released on surety for his appearance to be tried. The case having been considered, the Lords 'ordained Colin, Earl of Argyll, justice principal, to whom the said Duncan MacCoull MacFarlane was delivered, to retain and cause him to be kept in sure firmance that he escape not,' and direct the said Duncan to be ' put to the knowledge of an assize within the tolbooth of Stirling upon the 13th day of January next to come.'"

There is some confusion between the two Duncans. From the reference to the "umquhile Duncan MacFarlane," it would appear that the brother-german to Andrew of Arrochar had died, and that the two prisoners produced by the Earl of Montrose were the men referred to in the following entry :—

"Caution by Wm. Drummond of Myllynab in 500 merks, for Duncan MacFarlane and in 100 pounds for Malcolm MacGillevoray, his servant, that they will appear to be tried for art and part in the slaughter of ——— Ra, and will keep the peace meanwhile."

In 1585, under date Holyrood House, 20th January, the following order appears :—

"The King and his Council being informed that his good and peaceable subjects inhabiting the countries of the Lennox, Menteith, Stirlingshire and Strathearn are heavily oppressed by reif, stouth, sorning and other crimes, daily and nightly committed upon them by certain thieves, limmers and sorners, lately broken loose upon them from the braes of the country next adjacent, charge is given to a number of lairds, some twenty-eight in number, to attend the council on the 28th January, under pain of rebellion, to give information as to the repressing of these outrages."

"Andro McFarlan of the Arroquhair" is named second on the list, but apparently it was inconvenient for him to attend, for under date, Stirling Castle, 30th January, it is ordained that :—

"As Andrew MacFarlane of the Arrochar, James McCondoquhy MacFarlane in Illinvow, Malcolm Beg MacFarlane in Letter in Stragartnay, have not obeyed the summons to appear under pain of horning, it is now ordered that the penalty take effect."

In the Parliament acts of this year four MacFarlane lairds are named, those of Clackon, Dumford, Kirktown and Orquhart.

In the Parliament held July, 1587, no fewer than nineteen acts were passed " for the quieting and keeping in obedience of the disordered subjects, inhabitants of the Borders, Highlands and Isles." In one of these acts they are described as, " delighting in all mischiefs and most unnaturally and cruelly wasting, slaying, harrying and destroying their own neighbours, and native country people, taking occasion of the least trouble that may arise in the inner parts of the Realm, when they think that care and thought of the repressing of their insolence is in any way relaxed, to renew their most barbarous cruelties and godless oppressions."

In a roll of the names of the landlords and bailies of lands, dwelling on the Borders and in the Highlands, " where broken men have dwelt and presently dwell," to which one of these acts refers, are the names of the Lairds of Buchanan, MacFarlane of the Arrochar, Luss, MacAulay of Ardincaple, and in a " Roll of the Clans that have Captains, chiefs and chieftains on whom they depend, oftimes against the wills of their landlords, as well on the Borders as in the Highlands, and of some special persons or branches of the said Clans, ordained to be ratified in that Parliament, are the Buchanans, the MacFarlanes of the Arrochar, and the Clan Gregor."

THE COLQUHOUN FEUD.

We now come to the fierce feud which existed for a number of years with the Colquhouns. The raids by the MacFarlanes on the lands of Luss in the time of Duncan, the 13th Chief, already noted, were an outcome of the civil wars of the period. Colquhoun and MacFarlane were on opposite sides, Colquhoun being a Roman Catholic, and MacFarlane of the Reformed Faith. Duncan was of the faction of Lennox and Glencairn, while Colquhoun favoured that of Cardinal Beaton and the Regent Arran. Before the battle of Langside, however, both had embraced the same cause, that of the Regent Moray and the young king, afterwards James VI.

The strife in Andrew's time was, therefore, an entirely different matter. It was essentially a clan quarrel, an out-and-out "deadly feud" of the traditional type. The narrative of events is found in government and private documents, and we shall allow these to speak for themselves, with only occasional comment where the bias of such writers as Sir William Fraser appears to call for protest.

It is evident that the chief reason for the strife was "the slaughter of one of the Clan of MacFarlane, Humphrey MacFarlane, . . . committed by Sir Humphrey Colquhoun of Luss," but we have also in the traditional MacFarlane account of the Bannachra raid, of 1592, another cause, equally potent of offence, namely, the secret intrigue between Sir Humphrey and the wife of John MacFarlane o' that Ilk. As the raids, however, appear to have begun in 1590, the second offence may have been of the nature of "fuel to the fire."

In the Colquhoun claims for restitution in regard to the vast amount of property taken from them, by their neighbours, it is not easy to decide which property is claimed to have been taken in any particular year, the charges harking back continually to old grievances, but it is evident that fairly friendly relations subsisted between the two clans immediately prior to the outbreak, for an agreement appears to have been reached in August, 1590. This seems to refer to the depredations by Duncan, the 13th Chief, and Walter of Ardleish.

Sir Wm. Fraser's account of this agreement is as follows :—

"The outstanding family quarrel between the Colquhouns and the MacFarlanes, which in the time of Sir John Colquhoun had been so fatal to many of

the dependents of the house of Colquhoun, was renewed
in the closing years of the lifetime of Sir Humphrey,
14th of Colquhoun and 16th of Luss. The Mac-
Farlanes made many incursions into the glens of Luss,
and carried off much property. In these frequent
and destructive inroads they seem to have met with
little opposition.

In a decreet-arbitral, pronounced between Sir
Humphrey Colquhoun of Luss for himself and his
tenants on the one part, and Andrew MacFarlane of
Arrochar for himself, his sons, kin, and friends on the
other part, dated Edinburgh, 10th August, 1590, it
was discerned that there should be paid to Sir
Humphrey and his tenants, by Andrew MacFarlane of
Arrochar, 40 oxen, price of the piece £12 ; 60 kye,
price of the piece £8 ; and 10 horse, price of the piece
£13 6s. 8d.

These details are set out in an assignation (given
later) to Alexander Colquhoun of Luss by his tenants,
dated 6th January, 1602.

It is doubtful if Andrew carried out the terms of this
decree, for the MacFarlane raids began in that year and
continued through the next. Then in 1592 came the
big affair which culminated with the burning of
Bannachra castle, and the death of Sir Humphrey
Colquhoun. Fraser's account of this, as is to be
expected, differs materially from the traditional record
handed down in the Clan MacFarlane. That historian's
narrative is as follows :—

" In July, 1592, a body of the MacFarlanes and
MacGregors, descending from the mountains, committed extensive depredations upon the fertile fields of
Luss, which were now ripening for the harvest. To
repel the aggressors, Sir Humphrey collected together
a number of his vassals, and was joined by several
neighbouring landed proprietors. The hostile parties
met, and a sanguinary conflict, which lasted till
nightfall, ensued. Sir Humphrey's assailants were

OLD HOUSE IN ARROCHAR VILLAGE.   DEMOLISHED 1922.

Here resided Mr. Nicol MacFarlane, who has in his possession an old Claymore, found in the ruins of Eilean-a-vow Castle.

more than a match for him, and he was forced to retreat. He betook himself to the castle of Bannachra, a stronghold, which had been erected by the Colquhouns at the foot of the north side of the hill of Bennibuie, at the south end of the parish of Luss. But here the knight did not find the shelter he expected. A party of the MacFarlanes and MacGregors pursued him, and laid siege to his castle. One of the servants, who attended the knight, was of the same surname as himself. He had been tampered with by the assailants of his master, and he treacherously made him their victim. The servant, while conducting his master to his room, up a winding stair of the castle, made him, by preconcert, a mark for the arrows of the Clan who pursued him, by throwing the glare of a paper torch upon his person, when opposite a loophole. This afforded a ready aim to the besiegers, whose best bowmen watched for the opportunity. A winged arrow darted from its string with a steady aim, pierced the unhappy knight to the heart, and he fell dead on the spot. The fatal loophole is still pointed out, but the stair, like its unfortunate lord, has crumbled into dust.

"Not content with the murder of the Lord of Bannachra, his merciless assailants also murdered three of his servants, Robert Colquhoun of Tullichin-taull, John Galloway, and Gavin MacLellan. And so little regard did these savage freebooters pay to the laws of chivalry that they brutally assaulted Jean Colquhoun, the fair and helpless daughter of Sir Humphrey.

"Having wreaked their vengeance on the inmates of the castle of Bannachra, they next set fire to the castle itself."

To the fatal battle of Bannachra Sir Walter Scott refers, in the Lady of the Lake, in the lines :—

" Proudly our pibroch has thrilled in Glen Fruin,
And Bannachra's groans to our slogan replied."

" The main facts of this tragic scene are proved by
two entries in the Records of the Privy Council,
several years after the events. On 31st December,
1608, Parlane MacWalter of Auchenvenell became
surety for Dougall MacCoull MacFarlane, sometime in
Drumfad and now in Tullichintaull, that he should
appear on the third day of the next Justice-aire of the
sherriffdom of Dumbarton, to underlie the law for the
alleged crimes following ; namely, for the alleged
coming to the place of Bannachra, pertaining to the
deceased Sir Humphrey Colquhoun of Luss, in the
month of July, 1592, besieging of the said house of
Bannachra, and raising of fire and burning thereof, and
for the slaughter of Sir Humphrey Colquhoun, and
ravishing of Jean Colquhoun, his eldest daughter.

" The other entry in the Records of the Privy Council,
on 13th January, 1614, shows that John, Earl of Mar,
became surety for John MacFarlane (son of Andrew,
14th Chief), now of Arrochar, that he should appear
and answer for the same crimes as those specified in the
preceding entry. A contract which was entered into
between Alexander Colquhoun of Luss and Malcolm
MacFarlane (of Gartartan) in 1603, also shows that
the MacFarlanes were accused of being art and part
in the murder of Sir Humphrey Colquhoun and his
three servants."

*   *   *   *   *   *

" While it is plain how Sir Humphrey was assassinated,
it is unknown by whose hand the deadly arrow was
actually shot. A contemporary chronicler (Robert
Birrell, a Burgess of Edinburgh) has noted in a diary
of events that happened in his time, which he recorded
just as they occurred, that on ' November 30th (1592),
John Colquhoun was beheaded at the Cross of Edinburgh, for murdering of his own brother, the Laird of
Luss.' The painful charge against John Colquhoun of
imbruing his hands in his brother's blood, rests on the
authority of Birrell alone (an authority which Fraser, in

other connections, accepts without cavil or dispute. —*Ed.*). The family papers afford no evidence of it. The retour of the service of Alexander Colquhoun, the younger brother of John, as heir to him, in several rents . . . . . which was expede on 11th February, 1607, and which states that John died in December, 1592, seems to corroborate so far the statement of Birrell as to the time of the death of John, the slight discrepancy as to the month being unimportant. . . . . It is possible that the statement of Birrell is inaccurate to this extent, that he should have recorded that the John Colquhoun who was executed was the servant, instead of the brother, of the Laird of Luss, the brother having died in the following month; as we know that a servant of the name of Colquhoun was accessory to the murder; and it is certainly very improbable that, in a fierce feud between the family of Colquhoun and the MacFarlanes, the next brother of the Chief of the Colquhouns would voluntarily take part with the enemies of his house against his own brother and Chief, and actually shoot him dead with his own hand.

"In the conflict which led to the death of Sir Humphrey, the Colquhouns were overpowered, and were entirely at the mercy of the victors. As they bribed the servant of the vanquished to accomplish the death of the Chief, and also assaulted his innocent daughter, and burned the castle, it is also probable that they may have captured John Colquhoun, the brother, and forced him to assist in the murder of his brother, Sir Humphrey, in such a manner as to make him responsible for that crime, and save themselves, as there is no trace that any MacFarlane or MacGregor suffered at the same time with John Colquhoun."

It will be seen that Fraser is at great pains to explain away this damning evidence to the extent, it seems to us, of making himself ridiculous. We shall leave his ingenuous statement to the judgment of our readers. We are grateful, however, to the worthy burgess,

Birrell, of Edinburgh, for keeping a diary. A judge once remarked, " Fools keep diaries," but this fool, we are prone to think, was justified in his folly.

Fraser, throughout his writings on behalf of the Colquhouns, is thorough paced in his condemnation of the MacFarlanes. Thieves, robbers, murderers— the words flow from his pen with unction. His indignation could not have been greater had he been himself a Colquhoun ; but when he is bound to record doubtful practices indulged in by the same John, they become merely boyish pranks, reprehensible certainly, but not to be regarded seriously, as for instance, " John, it would appear, had acquired notoriety by his adventures in harassing and despoiling the tenants of neighbouring lands." These adventures (sic) included a cart horse worth 20 pounds stolen from John Dennistoun of Colgrain, and a grey horse and a dun grey mare from the widow of Patrick Lawrie of Colgrain. He also stole a brown horse of the value of £20 from the brother of the widow, as well as a grey mare worth £16, while, from Camiseskan, he " lifted " two cows and six sheep.

But Fraser's picture was to the order of his patron, Sir James Colquhoun, and he must needs paint with a white brush.

Disguise the fact as he may, John Colquhoun was what we would call " a bad lot," and may well have killed his brother. He was the cause also of a feud between the Galbraiths and Colquhouns by killing Donald MacNeill MacFarlane, household servant of Robert Galbraith of Culcreuch. The following is the reference :—

In 1593 Galbraith obtained a commission of justiciary for pursuing the Clan Gregor, which involved power to convene the lieges. Alexander Colquhoun, 15th of Colquhoun and 17th of Luss, and Aulay MacAulay of Ardincaple, however, suspected that Galbraith had really secured this power to extend his malice against them, and, "under the pretext of searching for MacGregors, to besiege and burn their houses." They accordingly complained that Galbraith had already given proof of such an intention by raising the Buchanans against Ardincaple, also the deadly feud betwixt Alexander Colquhoun of Luss and Galbraith, by reason of the slaughter of the deceased Donald MacNeill MacFarlane, household servant to Robert Galbraith, committed by Alexander Colquhoun's late brother, still stood between their houses, unreconciled, and the Laird of Culcreuch was daily awaiting for opportunities to avenge that slaughter. On these and other grounds, Colquhoun and MacAulay were exempted from the duty of pursuing the Mac-Gregors on that occasion.

As this Alexander, the third son of Sir John Colquhoun, succeeded his brother—he was laird in the year following the Bannachra affair (1593)—there seems little doubt that it was, in truth, John, the brother of Sir Humphrey, and not, " a gillie of that name," who was executed in Edinburgh in 1592. And who more likely to suborn the traitor Colquhoun than a Colquhoun. Certainly, if there was any suborning it was more likely to be the work of John Colquhoun than John MacFarlane. The circumstantial account of the Bannachra raid, given by the Rev. James Dewar, seems to be much more probable, especially in regard to the Colquhoun traitor. Fraser's elaborately conceived plot for the killing of Sir Humphrey is altogether a tax upon our credulity. It is not reasonable to suppose that such a plan could be formed in the course of a short retreat and pursuit. There was so much against the particular circumstances arising which necessarily had to be anticipated.

But whatever hand John Colquhoun had in the slaughter of his brother, historians and antiquarians persist in charging the death of Sir Humphrey Colquhoun upon the Clan MacFarlane. They do

not, however, agree as to the time and circumstance,
some asserting it to have been done upon the evening
of the bloody slaughter of Glenfruin, after the victory
over the Colquhouns in 1603.   Buchanan for instance,
writes :—" The Laird of Luss having escaped from the
battle was afterwards killed by the MacFarlanes
through the influence of a certain nobleman whom
Colquhoun had disobliged," and Sir Walter Scott
accepts Buchanan's version ; but the inviolable
tradition as handed down in the MacFarlane family
and written down by the Rev. James Dewar, M.A.,
when minister of Arrochar, appears to us to be nearest
the truth.

THE RAID OF GLEN FINLAS.

Mr. Dewar's narrative runs as follows :—" In the
reign of James VI., MacFarlane's dwelling-house was
at Tarbet, on the shores of Loch Lomond, close to
where the school-house now stands.   At that time,
when the taking of cattle from the Lowlanders
was a gentlemanly occupation, MacFarlane levied
the ' blackmail' for the rent of the Earl of Lennox's
land, and protected the tenants from robbers.   He
had a band of one hundred men living between Loch
Sloy and Tarbet, ready to arm at the shortest notice.
He (John, afterwards 15th chief) was married to a lady
by name Buchanan of Kilmaronock.   She, as was the
custom in that day, spun and made webs of cloth.
Her weaver lived at Banairich, a mile below Luss.
She often had an excuse to go to his house.   There
were no roads then, and when she went, it was by boat.
Reports of her improper intimacy with Sir Humphrey
Colquhoun had reached MacFarlane, and his jealousy
was aroused.   On one occasion she wished to go to her
weaver's with a web.   MacFarlane was unwilling to
allow her, and desired her to send a servant instead,
but she would not listen to his request, and as she was
hastily dressing, a note fell from her garments, which

her husband lifted, unperceived by her. On reading
the paper, he found it contained an arrangement for
the meeting, that day, of his lady and Sir Humphrey
Colquhoun.

"After she had left, MacFarlane aroused his ' Air-
phi,' and marched them down by the most direct road,
across Glen Douglas. They crossed Luss Glen at
Auchengarna, came through the wood above
Banaridhu, and surrounded the house. They could
see Mrs. MacFarlane and Sir Humphrey walking
together. He understood that the MacFarlanes had
not come as friends, and fled for refuge to his castle of
Bannachra, about five miles distant, and outrunning
his pursuers, had all the doors secured before they
came up. The MacFarlanes were unable to force the
doors, nor did they know in what part of the castle
he was concealed, but finding Sir Humphrey's body-
servant in an outhouse, they brought him to Mac-
Farlane, who put his sword to the servant's breast,
saying, ' Tell me in what part of the castle your master
is concealed, or I will run this sword through you.'
The poor wretch, thus threatened, told where Sir
Humphrey was hidden, when MacFarlane caused his
men to bring brush, heather and wood and set fire
to them on the windy side of the castle.

" The smoke forced Sir Humphrey to open a window
for breath, when one of MacFarlane's men shot him
with an arrow that gave him a mortal wound. The
doors were then opened, and Sir Humphrey was
delivered into MacFarlane's hands, who caused him to
be beheaded at once, and the body mutilated in
revenge."

In returning, they took the gates of the castle of
Ross Dhu, which were of iron, with them, and carried
them to Arrochar, where they remained in the
possession of the MacFarlanes until the estate was sold
to Ferguson of Wraith in the year 1784.

Mrs. MacFarlane had a bill of divorce served upon

her, and leaving Arrochar, she went to live with her relatives. Some time thereafter, Sir Humphrey's successor requested MacFarlane to send back the gates. He replied : " If you want the gates, come and take them away."

Soon Colquhoun of Luss collected his men and came up through the " String of Luss " to revenge himself on MacFarlane, and to recover the old gates of his castle. The Arrochar people did not expect them, and Colquhoun came upon them unawares.

MacFarlane and MacFarlane of Gartartan were in his house, drinking ale, when they arrived. Mac-Farlane leaped from a back window and hid in the thicket. The Colquhouns searched the house, but while doing so the cry of " Loch Sloy " was sounded, and MacFarlane's men came to their chief's aid. MacFarlane led his gathered men. The Colquhouns stood on a common between where Tarbet House now stands and Glen Tarbet rivulet. The MacFarlanes were gathered on the opposite side, and the chiefs began to parley, but it soon became apparent that the MacFarlanes were too numerous for the Luss men, and the chief of the Colquhouns and his men hastily fled above the woods and along by Loch Lomond, where there was a foot-path, never again coming to claim the gates of Ross Dhu.

The gates, it is said, were kept at Tighvechtan, " The House of the Watch," in Tarbet Glen."

It will be observed that Fraser omits all reference to Ross Dhu, although in Colquhoun's claim, dated 1603, against Andrew MacFarlane is mention of damage done to, "the manor place and fortilice of Rossdhu."

The brutal assault upon Jean Colquhoun, mentioned by Fraser, tends also to confirm the accuracy of the Arrochar tradition. To men of those times " an eye for an eye and a tooth for a tooth " was simple justice.

It seems rather superfluous in the circumstances for Alexander Colquhoun, on 8th May, 1593, to bind

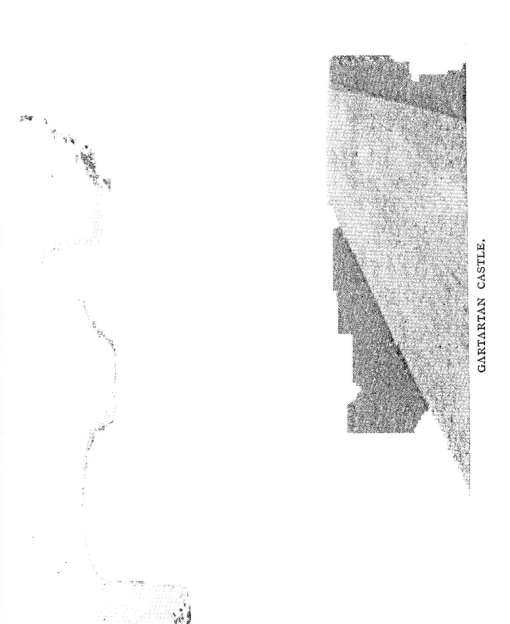

GARTARTAN CASTLE.

himself not to harbour or protect any of the surname of MacFarlane, under pain of £2,000 Scots, but this was merely a case of the new laird putting his signature to a general bond of 1587, which was directed also against the Buchanans and MacGregors. Robert Erskine of Sauchie having become surety, on 13th September, 1593, that Andrew MacFarlane of Arrochar, his men, tenants and servants, for whom he was answerable, should satisfy persons scathed. Alexr. Colquhoun, by making the usual charges of the MacFarlanes having at divers times committed robberies, thefts, hardships, incursions, depredations, and oppressions upon the people of Luss, without, be it remarked, giving the reasons for the same, the Colquhoun Chief obtained letters of prohibition under the Royal Signet, 12th December, 1593, addressed to the sheriffs of Stirling, charging them to prohibit the said Robert Erskine from selling, alienating, and disposing of any of his lands, heritages, corns, cattle, goods, or gear, and to prohibit, by open proclamation, at the market cross of Stirling and other places needful, the lieges from buying, receiving, or taking in " woadset " from the said Robert any of his (Colquhoun's) lands, etc.

Adam Colquhoun of Milton, in like manner, brought an action of contravention against Wm. Cunningham of Polmaise, who had become a cautioner for the MacFarlanes, before the Lords of Session ; and on 1st March, 1595, he obtained a decree, decerning that the MacFarlanes had been guilty, as charged by the complainer, and that William Cunningham had incurred the pains contained in the act of cautionary, and that therefore, he should pay the one-half of these pains to his Majesty, and the other half to Adam Colquhoun, the party aggrieved.

It was on 21st March, 1590, that Wm. Cunningham became cautioner with regard to Letters of Lawborrows (legal security) registered in the Books of Secret Council for John MacFarlane, son and apparent heir of

F

Andrew MacFarlane of Arrochar, Andrew MacFarlane of Gartavartane, Malcolm, Andrew, and John Dow MacFarlane, his three sons, Malcolm Beg MacFarlane in the Letter, and Walter MacFarlane, his son, that Adam Colquhoun in Milton, his wife, bairns, tenants, and servants, should be harmless and skaithless in their bodies, lands, possessions, and goods, under various penalties. John MacFarlane, apparent of Arrochar, under the pain of 5,000 merks, Andrew MacFarlane of Gartavartane, under the pain of 1,000 merks, and each of the other persons mentioned under the pain of 300 merks. It was claimed by Colquhoun that the MacFarlanes had contravened, on divers occasions, the said Act of Cautionary. Adam Colquhoun raised this action, and William Cunningham was condemned to pay the aforesaid penalties.

On 23rd December, 1595, a charge was directed against a considerable number of persons, under deadly feud, nobles, knights, barons, and others to appear personally before the King and Council at Holyroodhouse, to underly such order as should be prescribed touching the removal of these feuds, and various efforts were made to restore harmony between the MacFarlanes and the Colquhouns. As a result a truce appears to have been made. In 1597 the Laird of Luss received from John Erskine, Earl of Mar, a bond assuring him that he and his tenants would remain unmolested by the MacFarlanes. It reads :—

" Be it known to all men by these presents, we John, Earl of Mar, Lord Erskine, for ourself, and taking the burden upon us for Andrew MacFarlane of Arrochar, John MacFarlane his eldest son, fiar thereof, Andrew MacFarlane of Gartavartane, Malcolm MacFarlane, his eldest son, fiar thereof, and the remaining surname of MacFarlane, our kin, friends, men, tenants, servants, dependents, assistants, partakers, and all others that are liable to undergo the law, desire to state and, by the tenour hereof, specially and expressly assure

Alexander Colquhoun of Luss, his kin, friends, men, etc., that they shall be unhurt, unharmed, unmolested, untroubled, uninvaded, or in any wise pursued, criminally or ' eiuilye,' in the law, or by the law, by me or our foresaid, for whatsoever cause, quarrel, or occasion bygone, preceding the date hereof, unto the 11th day of November next to come ; promising to observe, and cause these presents to be observed and kept inviolate in any point, under the pain of ' periurie,' infamy, and loss of perpetual credit, honour, and estimation, in time coming. In witness whereof, we, for our help, and taking the burden upon us, as said, subscribe these presents, as follows, at Stirling Castle, the first day of June, the year of God, fifteen hundred and ninety-seven, before these witnesses, Harry Shaw, Thomas Howme, Charles Panter and Andrew Buchanan, our servants.   J. MAR.

A. BUCHANAN, Witness.
THOMAS HOWME, Witness."

On the 7th of November, 1597, Alexander Colquhoun subscribed a similar bond, carrying the truce to a later date, namely, " unto the last of November instant."

The disturbances caused by these clan contentions in the South Highlands were a source of great uneasiness and anxiety to James VI. and his Government, so for the preservation of the peace, his Majesty and the lords of the Privy Council issued letters to the sheriffs requiring them to command the principal men within their jurisdiction to find sufficient sureties, to be registered in the Books of the Privy Council for their good behaviour.

Ludovic, Duke of Lennox, was appointed by His Majesty's Commissioner of Justiciary, within the shire of Dumbarton, regality and dukedom of Lennox, to carry out suitable measures. Apparently he made a determined effort to settle the many vexed questions amongst the Lennox Clans, but not with entire success.

In the Montrose Charter-chest is an undated paper to Ludovic, containing offers made and given in by John MacFarlane, fiar of Arrochar (eldest son of Andrew), and Malcolm MacFarlane, fiar of Gartavartane (third of Gartartan), with special consent of Andrew MacFarlane of Arrochar, and Andrew Dow MacFarlane of Gartavartane, their fathers, for themselves and their kin, friends, and surname, for whom they were answerable. They offer first, to satisfy all parties scathed by any of their deeds in time past, his Lordship assigning to them a reasonable day for that purpose; and, secondly, to find sufficient landed noblemen as cautioners and sureties for them in regard to the time to come, that they should compear before his Lordship, at his command, on a reasonable day, to answer for themselves and their friends foresaid, and to make satisfaction for any scathe that they might hereafter commit, and to deliver up the perpetrators, or else to banish them out of the bounds of Arrochar, and to give them no assistance, supply, or entertainment, either directly or indirectly. A concluding paragraph, however, leaves unsettled the feud with the Colquhouns.

There was to be no forgiving and forgetting, for the MacFarlanes say, " Last under protestation that these offers fasten nothing against them for any particulars, standing or committed, in times bygone, between them and the house of Luss, in respect of the deadly feud standing between them unreconciled, until the same be taken away. Otherwise they offer all that they may do in any way, their lives and lands being excepted, and pray his lordship to take some good order, therewith."

This appears to have been in the nature of a private communication. When the matter came to a public issue the MacFarlanes were still more cautious. They would only make restitution in proved cases of injustice. They, however, entered into the usual bonds, for what these were worth; very little, we are inclined to think.

At Glasgow, on 21st November, 1599, the Duke decided that the various landlords of the county, and generally all others, having broken men upon their lands and heritages, should find sufficient cautioners and sureties to his Lordship, that they and their men should be answerable to justice before his Lordship and his deputies, and give redress to parties who should be scathed.

The Chief of the Clan MacFarlane declared that they were not able to find the said caution, but offered to make restitution of all bygone theft, reif, and oppression so far as the parties that had sustained loss were able to make proof thereof. His Lordship therefore, at the same meeting, in order to the settlement of such questions, ordained that the party who was scathed should elect a number of honest men, not exceeding 16 persons, dwelling within the shire of Dumbarton and regality of Lennox, " or four halves about," and that the person accused of committing the crime, should, out of this number, choose the one-half, as a jury, by whose verdict he should either be exculpated, or sentenced to refund the scathe that had been done.

For refunding that loss John MacFarlane, fiar of Arrochar, and Malcolm Dow MacFarlane of Gartavartane, as principals for themselves and their clan and surname of MacFarlane, were to find sufficient cautioners, in so far as they had not been already found; and that good order might be the better kept in future by the clan and surname of MacFarlane, it was ordained that the said John and Malcolm MacFarlane should be warded by the said noble lord until satisfaction should be made by them or their cautioners for the said bygone scathe, which should be done before the 1st of March following, and also until the said John and Malcolm found sufficient cautioners, under the pain of 5,000 merks ; John, 3,000 and Malcolm, 2,000 ; that they, their said clan and surname, should abstain forthwith from all theft and oppression in time coming, and should refund the scathe that should happen to be committed by any of them to the person damaged, upon its being proven.   It was further ordained that the said John and Malcolm should enter the committers of the said crimes prisoners for trial by the said noble lord, or should banish them forthwith from the bounds over which they had authority, and that should the principals, when they had opportunity, neglect to apprehend them before their banishment, or harbour or maintain the fugitives when they re-entered within the said bounds, or suffer to pass through their bounds any other thieves, clans, or oppressors, whom it might be in their power to prevent, they should be held culpable of the said crimes.

Soon after, John MacFarlane, fiar of Arrochar, and Malcolm MacFarlane, fiar of Gartavartane, appeared before Ludovic, Duke of Lennox for the purpose of giving the security required.   Sir Patrick Maxwell of Newark (John's grandfather) became cautioner for John, and David Cunningham of Ibert, Walter Leckie of Easter Poldar, and Wm. Graham of Doucheall (Duchray) (?), for Malcolm, binding themselves to present them before the Duke, within the Castle of Edinburgh, upon the 1st day of December, 1600, within the space of 15 days after his Lordship's letters were delivered to the parties for whom they were cautioners, under the pain of 5,000 merks, that the said persons might redress, " any enormities, reifs, thefts or scathes," that should be committed by them or those for whom they were answerable.

As we have suggested, the Colquhouns had small success with their law pleas, and in 1602 no restitution apparently having been made, they were, somewhat naturally, becoming impatient.   On the 6th of January of that year, Walter, James, and Adam Colquhoun, of Milton of Colquhoun, and others, assigned their claims against the MacFarlanes to their Chief, Alexander. These included the award already detailed of the

" decreet arbitral," of 1590, for the damage done in Duncan's time and some depredations of February, 1589; the horses, cows, oxen, and other goods and gear, wrongously taken away from them, out of their rooms and possessions, by Andrew MacFarlane of Arrochar, John MacFarlane, fiar of Arrochar, Humphrey Mac-Farlane, his brother, Malcolm MacFarlane of Gartavar-tane, and their accomplices.

The Chief of Colquhoun apparently took no action upon this assignation, for, on March 12th, 1603, a large number of the friends and dependents of the Laird of Luss—Colquhouns of Blairvaddich, Kil-patrick, Kilmardinny, Camstradden, and Hill—obtained a decree of the Lords of Council and Session against Andrew MacFarlane of Arrochar and his two sons, John and Humphrey, commanding them to make restitution to the pursuers of certain goods, gear, inside plenishings, " abnilzeimentis " and other property of which they had wrongously despoiled them, and to make payment to them of the price and profit of the same, each to pay his own proportion, as is particularly expressed in the decree.

From a list preserved at Ross Dhu of the beasts, goods, and gear, taken by the MacFarlanes, from the Laird of Luss and his tenants in the years 1590 to 1594, an idea can be found of the vast nature of the despoiling.

Below we give the details of the four years, in respect to the animals " lifted."

1590.

	£	s.	d.
5 Horses,	£126	6	8
2 Staiggis,	20	0	0
21 Mares and 11 Foals,	625	6	8
21 Cows,	248	0	0
5 Oxen,	62	0	0
20 Sheep,	25	0	0
Carried forward,	£1,106	13	4

1591.

	£	s.	d.
Brought forward, - - -	£1,106	13	4
8 Horses, - - - - -	£148	0	0
2 Staiggis, - - - - -	20	0	0
15 Mares and 3 Foals, - - -	197	6	8
26 Cows, - - - - -	322	13	4
11 Oxen, - - - - -	138	0	0
68 Sheep, - - - - -	102	0	0

1592.

	£	s.	d.
7 Horses, - - - - -	£436	0	0
2 Staiggis, - - - - -	26	13	4
13 Mares and 5 Foals, - - -	262	0	0
34 Cows, - - - - -	357	0	0
10 Oxen, - - - - -	140	0	0
44 Sheep, - - - - -	98	0	0

1593.

	£	s.	d.
1 Horse, - - - - -	£20	0	0
1 Stag, - - - - - -	10	0	0
3 Mares, - - - - -	36	13	4
4 Cows, - - - - -	46	0	0
4 Oxen, - - - - -	56	0	0
8 Sheep, - - - - -	12	0	0

1594.

	£	s.	d.
4 Horses, - - - - -	£96	13	4
1 Stag, - - - - - -	6	13	4
20 Mares, - - - - -	197	13	4
37 Cows, - - - - -	385	0	0
10 Oxen, - - - - -	132	0	0
24 Sheep, - - - - -	21	0	0
	£4,371	0	0

The summons also contains a statement of the profits lost by the theft of the animals in the five years, from the time of theft to the date of the summons. The whole amount claimed is £155,501 8s.

The above list is, of course, exclusive of the " inside gear," *i.e.*, household furniture and other goods taken.

A few months later the various Colquhoun claimants, apparently for the second time, assigned their claims to their Chief. It will be observed that in the summons above referred to, only the Arrochar MacFarlanes are named, Andrew the Chief and his two sons, John and Humphrey. The explanation of this is that a little later in the year a reconciliation, probably then pending, was effected between the Colquhouns and the Gartartan MacFarlanes. This rather seems to indicate that John and Malcolm, the eldest sons of Arrochar and Gartartan, were not acting in the same cordial unison as before. At all events, a bond was entered into between Alexander Colquhoun and Malcolm MacFarlane, apparent heir of Gartavartane, for himself, and in name of his brothers, his father's brothers, and the sons of his father's brothers. This bond confirms that the MacFarlanes were art and part in the slaughter of Sir Humphrey and his three servants.

Alexander Colquhoun bound himself to stop proceedings against Malcolm MacFarlane and those whom he represented, on account of these slaughters, and to grant them a remission for the spoilations and thefts which they had committed at Colquhoun, Connaltown, Tullychewan, the manor place and fortalice of Ross Dhu, on his brother, Sir Humphrey, himself, and their tenants. On the other hand, Malcolm became bound to grant a bond of manrent and service to Alexander Colquhoun, himself, and his friends, against all men, except the Duke of Lennox ; and engaged, should that bond be contravened by himself personally, to pay to Alexander Colquhoun 5,000 merks, and should it be contravened by others, to deliver up the contravenors to Alexander, and failing which, to pay to him for every contravention, 1,000 merks. It was further stipulated that this agreement in no way affected the claims of the Laird of Luss against Andrew MacFarlane, Laird of Arrochar and his sons, John and Humphrey, and their friends, for their part in these crimes.

·One reason why the Colquhouns suffered so seriously at this time without being in a position to pay back in kind, was probably the fact that all their neighbours to the north and west, MacGregors, MacAulays, Mac-Farlanes, and Campbells, were more or less in league against them. Besides, the MacFarlanes, the Duke of Argyll, and the Clan MacGregor had reasons of their own for attacking the Colquhouns. The lands of Luss, indeed, suffered more at the hands of the MacGregors than even at those of the MacFarlanes. These invasions culminated in the Raid of Glenfinlas, 17th December, 1602, and the historic battle of Glenfruin, 7th February, 1603.

Just as the MacGregors assisted the MacFarlanes in the Bannachra raid of 1592, so apparently John MacFarlane, the heir apparent of Arrochar, lent his strength to the MacGregor enterprise*. Dougall MacCoull MacFarlane, sometime in Drumfad and afterwards in Tullichintaull, whom we have already mentioned as being indicted in respect to the Bannachra affair with John MacFarlane, afterwards of Arrochar, were accused of " being in the company with the late Alastair MacGregor of Glenstra, his kin and friends at the field of Glenfruin."

In a note to " Rob Roy," in allusion to the murder of the students from Dumbarton College, who came to witness the battle of Glen Fruin, Sir Walter Scott wrote :—

" An ancient and constant tradition preserved among the inhabitants of Dumbartonshire, and particularly those of the Clan MacFarlane, relieves Dugald Ciar Mor (ancestor of Rob Roy) of the guilt of murdering a party of students for clerical orders from Dumbarton who had imprudently come out to witness the battle.

* Readers of " The Red Fox " should note that in that novel, for narrative purposes, the three invasions are made to appear as if one, and that apocryphal event ante-dated to the previous reign. [Ed.]

The MacFarlane legend attributes the blame to a certain Donald or Duncan Lean, who performed the act of cruelty with the assistance of a gillie who attended him, named Charlioch, or Charlie. They say that the homicides dared not again join the clan, but that they resided in a wild and solitary state as outlaws in an unfrequented part of the MacFarlanes' territory. Here they lived for some time undisturbed, till they committed an act of brutal violence on two defenceless women, a mother and daughter of the MacFarlane Clan. In revenge of this atrocity the MacFarlanes hunted them down and shot them. It is said that the younger ruffian, Charlioch, might have escaped, being remarkably swift of foot. But his crime became his punishment, for the female whom he had outraged had defended herself desperately and had stabbed him with his own dirk in the thigh. He was lame from the wound and was the more easily overtaken and killed."

As is well known, after this battle the MacGregors were proscribed and harassed upon all sides. In 1611 their chief refuge was an island of Loch Katrine, where they accumulated warlike stores and food supplies. It was necessary therefore that the Government in its determination to extirpate the clan should attack by boat, and they proposed to transfer all " the boats and birlingis " upon Loch Lomond to Loch Katrine for this purpose. Accordingly the Privy Council issued an order, ordaining that all his Majesty's subjects betwixt sixteen and sixty years of age, within the shire of Dumbarton, Stewartry of Menteith, and six parishes of the Lennox, in the Shire of Stirling, should be summoned by open proclamation at the market cross of Dumbarton, Stirling, Doune and Menteith to meet at the head of Loch Lomond on the 12th of February, 1611, for the purpose of carrying the boats and birlings which were upon Loch Lomond to Loch Katrine.

Meantime Colquhoun, exasperated by his great loss

at the battle of Glen Fruin, was preparing personally
to head an attack upon the outlawed clan. On the
31st of January, 1611, he appeared at Stirling before
the Privy Council in company with John, Earl of Tulli-
bardine, William, Lord Murray, his son Henry, Lord
St. Colme, Sir Duncan Campbell of Glenurquhy, knight,
Sir George Buchanan of that Ilk, James Campbell of
Lawers, and Andrew MacFarlane of Arrochar. Each
of them undertook, " to go to the fields and to enter
into action and blood against " the Clan Gregor
between that date and the 13th of February following,
and to prosecute that service for a month at his own
charges. Thereafter the King was to defray the
expenses of the maintenance of 100 men to assist them,
whilst they were to bear the cost of another 100 men
until the service should be ended. At the same time
Duncan Campbell, Captain of Carrick, was required to
remove all boats out of Loch Long and Loch Goil, that
the Clan Gregor might have no passage on these
lochs.

The appearance of Andrew MacFarlane in the
company of the laird of Colquhoun indicates that the
feud between the two clans had at last been reconciled.
We have not been able to trace how this was brought
about, but the settlement was effected before 1610, as
appears by a decree of the Lords of Council of 15th
February of that year. In introducing this item of
history, Fraser has the grace, at last, to say, " The
cause of this feud was the slaughter of one of the Clan
MacFarlane, Humphrey MacFarlane, father of John
MacDouill Vic Neill MacFarlane, committed by Sir
Humphrey Colquhoun."

The decree of the Lords of Council acquits Alexander
Colquhoun of Luss from an action raised against him,
at the instance of Gillemor MacIlerith, in Little Hills,
Glen, who had summoned him to exhibit, personally,
before the Lords of Secret Council on 15th February,
1610, John MacDouill Vic Neill MacFarlane, who, on

8th January preceding had been denounced rebel, and put to the horn, by virtue of letters raised at the instance of Gillemor MacIlerith, for not finding sufficient caution acted in the books of adjournal for his personal appearance before the justice and his deputies on a certain day bygone, to have submitted himself to the law for the cruel murder and slaughter of the said Gillemor's daughter, Catherine, committed by him.

Alexander Colquhoun was summoned to exhibit the said John MacDouill Vic Neill MacFarlane, because that person was his tenant and servant, dwelling in the lands of Shemore Glenfinlas, and for whom, therefore, it was affirmed, he ought by the laws of the realm, acts of Parliament, and general bond, to answer, and whom he should present for trial. The decree is in the following terms :—

" The Lords of Secret Council acquit completely the said Alexander Colquhoun of Luss from the prosecution and petition of the said pursuer in this matter, and from all the points, clauses and articles contended in the said summons and find him free therefrom in time coming, because the said Lords understand that deadly feud and enmity, which was of long continuance between the said Alexander Colquhoun of Luss, his kin and friends on the one part, and the Clan Farlane on the other part, which existed upon the occasion of the slaughter of Humphrey MacFarlane, father to the said John MacDouill Vic Neill MacFarlane and was committed by Sir Humphrey Colquhoun of Luss, brother of the said Alexander Colquhoun of Luss, is now by the King Majesty's special direction reconciled and agreed, and the barbarous and detestible cruelties which fell out upon the occasion of that feud altogether removed, and that the exhibition of the said John MacDouill MacFarlane will not only give occasion to revive and renew the said feud but will cause great trouble and disquiet in the country, and also because

Andrew MacFarlane of Arrochar, Chief and Chieftain of the whole Clan Farlane, has found caution and surety for making of all those persons for whom he is held to answer, obedient and answerable to justice, conformable to the laws of this realm, acts of Parliament, and general bond, and that the said pursuer may have good action against the said Andrew MacFarlane as Chief and Chieftain of the clan, and against his cautioners for the exhibition of the said John MacDouill Vic Neill MacFarlane who is one of the branches of the said clan, and in the revenge of whose father's slaughter committed by the said Sir Humphrey Colquhoun of Luss, the whole clan assisted and took part.   For the which causes the said Lords acquit the said Alexander Colquhoun of Luss in the manner aforesaid."

Fraser, or rather one of his ghosts (see Preface), adds : " The facts recorded in this decree go far to explain the cause of the violent depredations committed by the clan of MacFarlane upon the lands and tenants of the Laird of Luss in the year 1590, and in subsequent years."

Harking back a little we find it stated that in 1608 the Clan MacFarlane were declared rebels at law, and that may have had an influence upon the final composition of the deadly feud.

The " plantation of Ulster " of 1608-10 we believe accounts for the settlements of MacFarlanes in the North of Ireland, particularly in County Tyrone.   The king (James VI.) adopted the experiment which on a smaller scale he had tried in the island of Lewis.   The Province of Ulster was to be sub-divided into lots, and offered on certain conditions to colonists from Scotland and England.   In March 1609, there came a letter to the Scottish Privy Council announcing the offer which His Majesty, " out of his unspeakable love and tender affection," now made to his Scottish subjects. Seventy-seven Scots came forward as purchasers; and if their offer had been accepted, they would have possessed among them 147,000 acres of Irish land. A re-arrangement which was made the following year, however, diminished the number of candidates. When, in the autumn of 1610, the Plantation actually began, fifty-nine was the number of the favoured Scots, and 81,000 acres were to be set at their disposal. Of the fifty-nine, five were nobles—the Duke of Lennox (Ludovic, 2nd Duke and 17th Earl), his brother, Lord D'Aubigny (Esme Stewart, subsequently 3rd Duke and 18th Earl), the Earl of Abercorn, the Lord of Burley, and Lord Ochiltree. With the two heads of the Lennox family engaged in the enterprise, it is a fair inference that some of the MacFarlanes took advantage of this scheme and settled in Ulster. Others, of course, went at later times, but this event seems to suggest the first settlement of the MacFarlanes of Ulster, from whom so many American members of the clan are descended.

It will have been observed throughout our account of the Colquhoun feud that John, Andrew's eldest son and heir-apparent, figured much more prominently than the chief himself, and the reason of this was that in 1581 Andrew put him in possession of the lands of Arrochar, reserving to himself only the liferent of the said lands. At that date Andrew's age would be 37 years, and this course was probably taken as the clan, on account of the arduous nature of their warfare, required a younger leader. Be that as it may, on 30th May, 1581, John MacFarlane, son and heir apparent of Andrew MacFarlane of Arrochar, was on a precept of sasine by Esme, Earl of Lennox, invested in the lands of Arrochar MacGilchrist, in the Earldom of Lennox and shire of Dumbarton, between the rivulet of Nether Inveruglas and the rivulet of Trostane, by the resigna-tion of the said Andrew into the hands of the said noble

Lord, the lord superior, in favour of his son, John, the father reserving to himself the liferent of the said lands. Andrew we have seen was alive in 1611, but he died in that or the following year, and was most probably buried at Luss.

The chiefs of MacFarlane who were hereditary lords of the soil, apparently always regarded Luss as their parish, worshipped in its church, and were buried in its graveyard. John caused an ornate stone to be carved and erected over his ancestors' sepulchre. When the new church was erected by Sir James Colquhoun, the stone was removed and built into the north wall of the new church, appropriately facing towards Arrochar. Surmounted by a death's head and an hour glass with crossbones on one side and on the other a crossed scythe and spade, it bears this inscription :—

> Here is the place of burial
> appointit for the Lairds of
> Arroquhar, buildit by Johne
> Mackfarlan Laird thairof
> 1612.

> EFTER DEATHE
> REMAIMIS VERTEW
> MEMENTO MORI
> J. M. 1612.

It is highly probable that John had this stone carved and erected after laying his father's remains in the grave. Andrew was 67 or 68 when he died, and for some 64 or 65 years he was Chief of the Clan—a long reign.

Malcolm Beg MacFarlane of The Letter in Stragartney, seems to have been a person of importance in the time of Andrew, the 12th chief, as he was, along with his son, Walter, held accountable, with the heads of the Arrochar and Gartartan families, for the alleged mis-deeds of the Clan in 1585 and 1590. He was probably a younger son of Walter of Ardleish. Prior

Gravestone in Ballyhennan Burial Ground showing Chief's Coat of Arms.

Memorial Stone to Chiefs of MacFarlane in wall of Luss Church. Dated 1612.

Gravestone in Ballyhennan Burial Ground to John MacFarlane, Piper in Inverioch, 1730. Time of Walter, 20th Chief.

to that time, in 1580, he had apparently been appointed by the king keeper of the forest of Glenfinlas, but that office was taken from him as the following from The Red Book of Menteith shows :

" Letters by King James the Sixth, discharging Malcolm Beg MacFarlane from keeping of the forest of Glenfinlas—Holyrood House, 7th December, 1580. James, by the Grace of God, King of Scots, to our loved Thomas Wallace, Messenger, Messengers, Sherrifs in that part, 'coniunctlie' and surely, specially constituted, greeting : Forasmuch as it is understood by us and the lords of our Secret Council that, lately, upon the day of November last, bypast, Malcolm Beg MacFarlane, in Letter, upon sinister and wrong information made to us privately obtained our other letter, subscribed with our hand, without the advice of our Council, giving and granting him the custody and keeping of our wood and forest of Glenfinlas, with the deer, therein, for a certain space, as the same at length details ; and seeing the same, as we are surely informed, has 'tendit and tindis,' altogether to our great hurt and 'lesious,' as also understanding our trusty cousin and councillor Sir James Stewart of Doune, knight, and his predecessors are and have been heritably invested in proper form and heritage in the keeping of the said wood and forest, and has been in continual possession thereof, to this hour ; and willing that our said trusty cousin and councillor be in no wise hurt nor deprived in his right and place of the said wood, but rather fortified and assisted therein, for his better and surer preservation of the same, our will is therefore, and we charge you straitly and command, that incontinently these our letters shall pass, and in our name and authority command and charge the said Malcolm Beg MacFarlane, Andrew MacFarlane of that Ilk, and all other pretending keepers of our said wood and forest, to desist and cease from all further occupation, 'melling,' keeping, cutting, or intromitting with

G

our said wood and forest or any part thereof, within 24 hours next after they be charged by you thereto, under the pain of rebellion and putting of them to our horn, and if they fail therein, the said 24 hours being bypast, that you incontinently thereafter denounce the disobedience and rebellion, and put them to our horn, and escheet, and inbring all their movable goods to our use for their contemptiousness ; and such like, that you, in our name and authority pass to the Market Crosses of our burghs of Stirling, Perth, parish kirk at Port Kilmadok, and other places needful, and let there be open proclamation, prohibition, command, and charge to all and sundry of our lieges and subjects whom it affects, that they nor none of them take upon hand to do nor attempt anything contrary to the tenour of these our letters, nor to answer, obey, or acknowledge any other forester or keeper of our said wood than our said trusty cousin, heritable fiar, aforesaid, and his deputies, under all highest pain and charge that after may follow, certifying them, that if they do anything to the contrary, they shall be punished therefor with all vigour according to law and conform to justice, as you will answer to us thereupon ; the which to do we commit to you our full power by these our letters, you delivering them duly executed and endorsed again to the bearer, Gavin, under our signet and subscribed with our hand at Holyrood-house, the vii. day of December, and of our reign the xiii. year, 1580.

                                              " JAMES R.

" LENOX.   C. E. ERGYLL."

CHAPTER XVI.

JOHN—15TH CHIEF.
1612-1624.

Duke of Lennox.   *Scottish Rulers.*
LUDOVIC—2nd Duke   JAMES VI.,1567-1625.

JOHN assumed the government of Arrochar in 1612. The character of the son of the hero of Langside, is difficult to estimate. He comes down to us as a gentleman of great piety, but that must have been a development of his later years. In his prime, he was, without doubt, of a most fiery and dominant nature, fierce and hasty of temper. Probably many of our readers will agree with our estimate when they have read his chronicle, that he was soured early in life by his first unfortunate marriage, and that repentance and grace came to him with his fourth matrimonial venture.

John, as we have indicated, married four times. His first wife was Susanna, daughter of George Buchanan of that Ilk. She had no children, and as we have seen he divorced her. His second wife was Lady Helen Stewart, daughter of Francis, Earl of Bothwell, the madcap Earl. His heir, Walter, was born of that union. Thirdly, he married Elizabeth Campbell, a daughter of the family of Argyle, by whom he had four sons, Duncan, who died unmarried, Andrew of Drumfad, John, ancestor of the Glenralloch MacFarlanes, and George, ancestor of the MacFarlanes of Clachan. His fourth wife was Margaret, daughter of James Murray of Strowan and she had no children.

On the 13th June, 1614, John, Earl of Mar, became surety for John MacFarlane, "then of Arrochar," that he should appear on 3rd day of the next Justice-Aire of Dumbarton to underlie the law for the same crimes as have previously been mentioned.   Dougall MacCoull MacFarlane was also named and the indictment included some later liftings of Colquhoun cattle, to wit, " For stealing of 70 cows and oxen belonging to Alexander Colquhoun of Luss, Robert MacWalter, etc., from the lands of Glenmulloche, Immerstachin and Drum Macnilling, in the month of June, 1602.   Item, for the stealing of six score cows and oxen in the month of July, 1602, out of the lands of Glenfinglas, belonging to the said Alexander Colquhoun of Luss, John Laing, Thos. McGilfadrick, and Patrick Colquhoun."

Duncan, John's second son, seems to have taken after his father in his warlike proclivities as the following narrative from the manuscript of the Rev. James Dewar, M.A., bears out.

RAID OF THE ATHOL MEN

" The Athol men were sent by the Regent of Scotland, on more than one occasion, to pillage Arrochar, and several battles were fought between them and MacFarlane, not now on record.   On one occasion they had taken MacFarlane's cattle, and were about to drive them away from Arrochar.   He was at that time in his house on Eilean-a-vow, and knowing their superior numbers, did not deem it prudent to land and oppose them ;   his son, Duncan, proposed to row ashore and gather men enough to hold the Athol men in check that night, during which time the clan would be gathered.

" This met with the Chief's approval.   There was then a mill near Port Chapel, where a number of young men lounged who lived on the farmers of Ballnich. They were the sons of men who had been killed in battle, and were thus maintained.   When a farmer had a meal in the mill, they were privileged to take as much meal from each sack as they could lift between the open palms of their two hands, and carry to the door without scattering any ; if this happened, they must put the meal back in the sack.

" Duncan MacFarlane went and got these young men, but they were poorly armed. He knew that the Athol men would attempt the Ford of Dhuglas. So Duncan took his men there, and they put clothing on the stumps of trees, knowing it would be dark when the Athol men would pass the ford, and hoping by this stratagem to deceive them with regard to numbers. When the enemy came in sight, some of them were going round an eminence, as though they were a reinforcement, and others with bows and arrows, were behind the stumps, to frighten the Athol men, and defend the ford.

" When the enemy came up, they began to shoot at the clothed stumps, the MacFarlane men shooting their arrows back to them. They soon discovered them to be their own arrows. It was dark, and fearing an ambush, they did not attempt the ford, but retired up Strath-du-daning to a place called Grianach, three miles from Loch Sloy, where the Chief of the Mac-Farlane had hunting-houses. They went into one and spent the night, killing four cows and roasting the flesh for their suppers. They made merry with songs until late at night, when they laid down to sleep without posting sentinels.

" Duncan MacFarlane, with his men, was watching them, and when all was still, they tied the doors on the outside, and set fire to the house, burning it with all the Athol men in it. The forest about the house was also burned and much valuable timber destroyed.

" Duncan retired to Eilean-a-vow, and reported what he had done, but his father did not believe him, and sent two trusty messengers to reconnoitre, who returned, confirming Duncan's story. The father was so angry that he drove him from home, and he was ever after called Black Duncan.

" Among the ruins of the burned house were found sixty swords, many battle-axes and as many arrowheads as would fill a peck measure. Arrochar people long feared that the Athol men would come to be revenged, but they never again molested the Clan MacFarlane."

The account of these incidents by the Reverend H. S. Winchester differs somewhat from that of Mr. Dewar. Mr. Winchester writes :—

"Duncan was the instigator of a cruel deed which earned for him the name—given by his own father—' Donach dubh na dunach ' (*i.e.*, Black Duncan of the mischief). A message arrived one evening from the watcher at Tighvechtan (the watch house) that a number of Lochaber men laden with booty were approaching Glenloin. Duncan who got the message, kept the news to himself, and going to the meal mill at Portachuple, where the young men used to gather in the evenings, he selected twenty stout fellows and made for the ford at Coire-ghrogain. Arriving there before the Lochaber men, he dressed up the stump of a tree to represent a man in armour, while he himself stood concealed on a knoll near at hand with his men close behind him. By the time the Lochaber men came up, it was growing dark, and mistaking the dressed-up stump for the leader of a party which was about to contest the ford, they began shooting arrows at it. Duncan waited until he thought their stock of arrows must be pretty well exhausted, and then he and his men rushed towards the ford, picked up the arrows, and shot them back with telling effect.

" Deeming it vain to force the passage, the Lochaber men made a pretence of retiring, but really pursued their journey up the stream by a very rugged and difficult route on the south side. When they had rounded the head of Loch Sloy, and entered the valley beyond, seeing no trace of the foe, and being exhausted with their trying journey, they halted and partook of some food. The night was cold, and as no signs of pursuit could be seen or heard, they crept into a small wooden hut which then stood on the border of the forest of Scots firs which covered the country, and which was used for storing the winter's fuel. Duncan, however, had followed them, he had watched their movements at a safe distance, and after waiting until he felt sure that the tired Lochaber men must be fast asleep, he and his men crept stealthily to the hut, secured the door, and heaping dry brushwood around the wooden structure, set fire to the whole. The hut was soon in a blaze, and when daylight came, all that could be discovered of the Lochaber men was the heads of their axes, and the blades of their dirks. But the fire burnt more than the hut ; it caught the heather and the forest, and it swept everything before it, leaving scarcely a tree standing or a tuft of heather between Loch Sloy and Garabal marsh."

Fraser gives us yet another variation with an interesting sequel :—

" Glenfalloch, which bounds the barony of Arrochar on the North, was the natural pass for the people of Athole into Arrochar on their way to the lower grounds in Menteith and Stirling, and many anecdotes are still current among the inhabitants of Arrochar of the raids of the Athole men on their ancestors. On one occasion the Athole men made a descent on Arrochar, and plundered the castle of the MacFarlanes on Eilean-a-vow, in the absence of the Chief and his retainers. On the return of the MacFarlane Chief, Duncan Dhu, or Black Duncan, his son, pursued and overtook the invaders in a shooting lodge in Staduish, which is a glen between Loch Sloy and the river Falloch. While the men of Athole were enjoying themselves with their plunder, Duncan Dhu and his party fastened the door of the shooting lodge and set it on fire. The fire consumed both the lodge and the invaders, and spreading, it reduced to ashes a large tract of the native Scotch fir trees with which the mountains were then covered. Along these mountains roots of fir trees, charred with burning, are still quite common. The shepherds, in place of candles, use these charred stumps, which, from the rosin, similar to turpentine, contained in the wood, makes a very good light.

• "On hearing of the conflagration, the father of Black Duncan, who foresaw that the enemy would be avenged, said to him : ' A bloody son you'll be to me.' As he had foreboded, three of the Athole men, friends of those who were burned, returned to Arrochar to avenge their death. Proceeding in search of Duncan Dhu, they found him—though ignorant of who he was, as he was personally unknown to them— engaged in splitting a log of wood on an island in the bay near Doune, in Lochlomond, called Eilean-a-ghoar. They asked him whether he knew the whereabouts of Black Duncan for that day. ' If you are very anxious,' he answered, ' to see him, I will go and point out where he is, if you will only wait a little and assist me with my work,'—at the same time exacting from them an oath that they would never reveal his information. Direct-ing the Athole men to catch the log, which was partly split at one end, he made use of their strength in tearing it up, and while tightening the wedge, he struck it out of the log, which closed upon their hands, and held them fast like a vice. Having them now completely in his power, he vociferated, ' Here is Duncan Dhu ! What do you want with him ? ' He then coolly killed all the three men ; and from this desperate deed the small island is still called Eilean-a-Ghoar (the Bloody Island)."

Mr. Winchester gives us an account of another of Black Duncan's exploits in the Uglas valley, as follows :—

"Being informed that a small party were driving cattle up Glenloin, Black Duncan waited their arrival between the ford of Coire-Ghroggain and Loch Sloy, at the place where the foot-path passes between two

UGLAS WATER, LEAVING LOCH SLOY.

IN UPPER UGLAS VALLEY.

TAING WATER, STRONAFINE.

HEAD OF GLEN LOIN.

stones which meet at a few feet from the ground, so
that in passing through you have to bend forward in
order to prevent your head from striking the top of
this natural archway. Duncan and one of his men
took up their positions on each side of this narrow
passage, but quite concealed from those coming, and
as the head of each man appeared beyond the stones,
Duncan brought down his claymore with such force
and skill as to sever the head from the body, while his
companion pulled the body from the passage to keep
it clear. Several were thus despatched before those
behind perceived the stratagem, and then they were
attacked by Duncan and his men who lay in ambush,
and put to flight."

Apparently John, after his feud with the Colquhouns,
went to war with the Buchanans, for we read that in
1619, John Darleith, with many Colquhouns,
Drummonds, Lindsay of Balliol, Bunten of Ardoch,
Galloway in Kilmaronock, and others, assisted the
MacFarlanes in their feud with the Buchanans. This
may have been an outcome of the divorcing of his un-
faithful wife of that name, but as that event occurred
some 27 years previously it does not seem likely except
that Highland revenges were long nursed, waiting
opportunity.

On the 28th February, 1622, John MacFarlane of
Arrochar, with consent of Walter MacFarlane, his son
and heir-apparent, for certain sums of money paid to
him, sold to Andrew MacFarlane, lawful son of Andrew
M'Coull MacFarlane, Blairvyok, without reversion,
and confirmed to him, the lands of Gortane, in the
lordship and barony of Luss, parish of Roseneath, and
shire of Dumbarton, to be held of the granter and his
heirs-male.

John, as we have said, is stated to have been a
gentleman of great piety. "He built an almshouse at
Bruitford on the mainland opposite to his castle on the
island called Eilean-a-vow, for the reception of poor

passengers who might happen to require shelter in visiting or passing through the district. This he endowed with competent revenues to provide the travellers with all necessities and accommodation. On the front of the almshouse was handsomely cut in stone his armorial bearings, with party per pale, baron and femme, three mullets being the arms of Margaret Murray, his fourth wife.

' "The almshouse referred to no longer exists, although at a place opposite Eilean-a-vow, on the mainland, the wall tracks of a house can yet be traced. The spot is called Croit a' phuirt, generally pronounced Crutyforst or Crutafoorst. It means the croft of the landing, or where persons embark and disembark from a small boat."

In 1624, which may have been in John's time (he is said to have died towards the end of the reign of James VI., 1625), or that of his successor, many of the clan were tried and convicted of theft and robbery. Some were pardoned and a number were removed to the uplands of Aberdeenshire, and to Strathaven in Banffshire, where they assumed the names of Stewart, M'Condy, Greisck, MacInnes, MacJames, etc.

MacFarlane-Buchanan Vendetta.

One of those crimes which may have been an incident of the Buchanan feud already referred to is detailed in the records of the Court of Session of June 6th, 1623, under the title of, " Slaughter of Duncane MacFarlane by Buchanans." The young laird of MacFarlane referred to, we judge to have been Walter, John's eldest son and the next Chief. Shorn, as far as possible, of its archaic language, the record runs as follows :—

" The same day anent the accusation at the instance of Robert and Thomas MacFarlane as brothers to the late Duncan MacFarlane, son to the late Andrew MacFarlane of Bunessan, charging George Buchanan of Gartincaber, John Buchanan, his son ; Patrick

Buchanan, son of George Buchanan of Auchmar; John Beg Buchanan of Ballindewar, John Buchanan, his son; Thomas Buchanan of Drougie and Archibald Buchanan, his brother, to appear personally this day and place to underly the law before His Majesty's Justice for art and part in the slaughter of the said Duncan MacFarlane, committed upon the sixth day of April, 1622, within the toune of Kippienoche in Drummond in the Lennox, in the form and manner specified in the said accusation. Appearing personally the said Robert MacFarlane as brother with the young laird of MacFarlane, and Mr. David Primrose, Advocate as Prelor for them—and Sir William Oliphant of Newtoun, Knight Advocate to our sovereign Lord for his hienes intreis—and producing the said criminal charge duly executed and undersate upon all the defendants above stated and offer themselves ready to pursue, etc.—Together with Mr. Robert Nairn, Advocate, his Prelocutor, who produced a warrant and command to the Justice regarding the continuation of this diet to the 13th day of June, directed by the Lords of the Secret Council and subscribed by my Lord Chancellor of the date the 5th day of June, proceeding upon a supplication, etc., of the which supplication and warrant upon the back thereof the tenour is as follows :—

' My Lords of Secret Council, unto your Lordships we, your humble servants, discover and show (names of Buchanans again detailed) that while the 6th of June is appointed unto us for our appearance before the Justice to underly the law for the slaughter of the late Duncan MacFarlane, son to the late Andrew Moir MacFarlane in Kypnoche when the Justice intends to proceed against us in the said matter, but were your Lordships acquainted of a verity of the certain truth of this business, how and upon what occasion the slaughter fell out and what occasions of wrath and displeasure was given us therein we are persuaded that your Lordships in honour and justice would not think this prosecution to merit any favour.

' The truth is that the said deceased Andrew Moir MacFarlane during the whole course of his unhappy life was known to be a notorious thief and villain. Having stolen some goods from certain of his Majesty's good subjects in the Lennox, some four or five years since or thereby, and the said late William Buchanan, out of his true hatred and detestation of such thieving doings, having made some inquiries and having taken pains and trouble to find the goods, in the end traced them to have been stolen by the said late Andrew Moir MacFarlane, who by course of justice was compelled to make restitution. For this Andrew Moir MacFarlane conceived a deadly hatred and malice against the said deceased William Buchanan and resolved out of the pride and malice of his wicked heart to be revenged upon him after the most detestable and cruel manner that the heart of him could devise. Knowing that the gentleman was accustomed at times for his recreation and pastime to hunt on the moor above ' the Ducher, he chose that occasion to do his turns. Accompanied by his two sons and seven or eight utterly lawless villains, MacFarlane lay in wait for the gentleman. Buchanan came about eight o'clock in the morning without any company but four sporting dogs. The MacFarlanes seized him and bound him so that he could not stir.

" Having consulted together after what form and manner they should dispatch him, in the end they resolved that his presumption and malapertness in discovering the goods deserved an extraordinary and unaccustomed death by torture which they made him undergo, during the space of ten hours, in the following manner :—

' They bound him fast to a tree at the said hour of eight in the morning and every hour thereafter until six at night, making ten hours, they gave him three cruel stabs with a dirk in such parts of his body where the wounds would not be fatal. Having mangled him in this way with thirty strokes until the full number of ten hours was outrun they then gave the last deadly blow at the heart when he fell dead to the ground. Having stripped him naked, because his tongue was the instrument whereby as they alleged he had offended in enquiring out the hiding places of the goods, they cut his throat, took his tongue out of his head, slew his four dogs, cutting one of their tongues out and putting it in the gentleman's mouth and put his tongue in the dog's mouth. Not content with this atrocity, but the further to satisfy their inhuman and barbarous cruelty upon the naked corpse, they slit open his belly, took out his entrails and put them into one of the dogs and put the dogs entrails into the gentleman's body. So they left him lying naked and the four dogs about him. It was eight days ere he was found. For this detestable butchery and murder these villains being called to their trial before His Majesty's Justice they, ' took the crime upon them and passed to the horne,' where the said Andrew Moir remained to the hour of his death and the rest of his accomplices still remain. Against them your Lordship passed an ample commission for the pursuit of them with fire and sword.

' Where this detestable and more than barbarous murder should have bred in the heart and conscience of this villain some remorse and feeling for this sin and an abstinence and forbearance from all further impiety, yet the said Andrew continued in his accustomed trade of theft, reif and oppression and never could be reclaimed therefrom till the hour of his death. In his last theft, a little before his death, he stole an ox from me, the said George Buchanan, and carried the same to a house where he and his wife were accustomed to receive stolen goods. As soon as we learned of the theft of the ox we followed the trail, directly, towards the said house, and sent for the officer of the Earl of Perth to assist us in searching the houses thereabouts. The villain and his son being in the house before mentioned, began to fear capture. They thereupon disguised themselves in women's clothing and tried to escape without being perceived. We, thinking they kept not the ordinary pace of women and yet noways suspecting that they were the villains we sought, followed softly to observe which way they took.

'The said Duncan MacFarlane, looking over his shoulder and seeing that we followed him, turned and pointed a long hacquebut at us. He fired, but by the providence of God the gun misgave. With that he and his father drew their swords and drove in upon us with all their force. Before we could defend ourselves they gave me, the said George Buchanan, a deadly stroke and I fell senseless to the ground. The rest of my company thought I was a dead man. They wounded three others of us. Unable any longer to restrain ourselves, we took to our just and lawful defence, when the unhappy villain was justly slain, and his son, who unfortunately was in company with him and who made the first onset with his hacquebut, ere ever we knew who he was, was likewise killed.

'The father was killed for the murder aforesaid and he and his whole family are the most notorious villains of that clan. However it may be charged on the part of the young man that he was not accessory to the murder aforesaid and that he

should not be punished for his father's deed, it is
the truth that continually since the father was
declared a rebel for the murder aforesaid the said
Duncan and his son remained and attended upon
him, was art and part with him in all his thieving
and wicked deeds, and assisted and took part with
his father against us in our just and lawful defence,
was slain, at whose hykewalk that night the ox
aforesaid, stolen by the father and the son was
slain and eaten.

'This being the true and simple statement of
all that has passed in this business we humbly
present the same to your Lordships consideration
whereby your Lordships may perceive how
'misshantlie' and barbarously the innocent and
harmless gentleman was murdered and slain and
what was the ground and occasion of the subsequent slaughters.

'Since there is great likelihood of disorder
arising to the disturbance and breaking of the
peace of the country with the Clan MacFarlane
going about their private revenge and our friends,
on their part, being careful of their own defence,
we humbly beseech your Lordships to take such
course and order concerning this matter as your
Lordships shall think most fit for the peace of the
country, etc.

'Apud Halirnidhous, 6th June, 1623.'"

"The Lords ordain and command the Justice to
continue the diet, within written, to the 13th day of
June, and ordain their petitioners to make offers to the
party and to present the offer to the young laird of
MacFarlane if he be in the town, and to the special
friends attending this diet whom the said Lords ordain
to remain in Edinburgh until some decision be taken
for settling the matter within written and for the peace
and quietness of the country, etc."

CHAPTER XVII.

WALTER—16TH CHIEF.
1624-1664.

Dukes of Lennox.	Scottish Rulers.	
LUDOVIC, 2nd Duke.	JAMES VI.,	1567-1625.
ESME, 3rd Duke.	CHARLES I.,	1625-1649.
JAMES, 4th Duke.	THE COMMONWEALTH,	1649-1660.
	CHARLES II.,	1660-1685.

WALTER, the son of John, was a Cavalier, loyally devoted to the cause of the Stuarts. He suffered greatly for his attachment to Charles I., but no losses could shake his fidelity to his party. He was with "The Great Marquis" of Montrose in his hurricane campaign of 1644-45, and the wild pibroch of the Clan, "Thogail nam Bo" inspired the Royalists in many a Highland battle.

For joining the standard of Montrose, Walter was fined 3,000 merks Scots, but throughout the Commonwealth he remained an irreconcilable king's man. In Cromwell's time, he was twice besieged in his house, and his castle of Inveruglas was afterwards burned down by the English. In the burning of Inveruglas, several of the ancient writs of the family were consumed.

Walter married Margaret, a daughter of Sir James Semple of Beltrees, Renfrewshire, one of the gentlemen of the bedchamber to James VI., and who was Scottish Ambassador to the Court of England, in 1599. They had two sons and one daughter, John, who succeeded as 17th Chief, Andrew of Ardess, who succeeded as 18th Chief, and Giles who married Adam Colquhoun of Glens. Walter died in 1664.

The story of the "Burning of MacFarlane's Forest"

INVERUGLAS CASTLE.

occurred in Walter's time. From the date, 1640, this devoted Royalist was obviously the chief concerned, and the act of heroism is quite in accordance with his reputed character. The forest in question extended from Loch Lomond to Ben Laoigh. Twenty-five miles round, it was the favourite hunting ground of the Chiefs of MacFarlane.

The following is taken from Sir F. Dick Lander's " Wanderings in the Highlands." This narrative has been abridged from some fifty pages or more, and is taken from a letter written by William Charles MacFarlane of the Kenmore or Muckroy family in 1837 to his brother, Captain James Duncan MacFarlane. W. C. MacFarlane was then at St. Edmund's Hall, Oxford.

THE BURNING OF THE FOREST.

" One fair evening as the Laird was musing most enjoyably upon the hill looking upon Arroquar, Loch Long, and a fair forest extending some 25 miles, his attention was drawn to one Angus MacFarlane, head shepherd to the Laird, and the fair Ellen whom Angus was about to marry. She was weeping. The Laird, who ever wished to be the father of his people, enquired the cause of her grief ; she told him that it arose from a vision she had seen the previous evening, of the forest all burning, and by the dim glare had distinctly seen the figure of the Laird bearing on his shoulders the dead body of her beloved Angus.

" Now it happened that this evening Angus had left the castle to come and see his own dearie, Ellen. They had not long retired to rest when tidings were brought that the cattle were harried. Angus immediately suspected the Lochaber men of having committed this depredation, nor was he mistaken.

" As swift as an eagle, he pursued them and tracked them into the thickest fastnesses of the forest, and sent tidings to the Laird, who instantly ordered the Gathering to be played. ' Loch Sloy—Loch Sloy '

H

sounded on all sides, and his followers were soon about
him, and meeting Angus's messengers on the way, they
soon reached the spot where Angus was on the look out.
Seeing a figure move, the henchman was on the point
of firing, when MacFarlane held his hand and in an
undertone challenged the person as follows :—

" ' Where grew your bow and how is it drawn ? '

" ' It grew in the Isles of Loch Lomond, and is
drawn for Loch Sloy,' was the reply of the well known
voice of Angus.

" The Laird, who was a very brave and cautious
leader, and showed on the occasion his fitness for the
command of such a gallant band, gave such orders that
the hovel where the Lochaber men were resting, was
surrounded. Four of the bravest and most active
young men were sent forward to give timely intimation
of any movement of the enemy.

" On one occasion Angus was seen to draw his bow
in the direction of the Laird. He was instantly felled
by his too zealous kinsfolk on suspicion of treason, but
his quick eye had descried within a few paces of the
Laird a Lochaber man with his dirk drawn and ready
to plunge into the bosom of his Chief. The Lochaber
man fell at the Laird's feet, and Angus had thus the
satisfaction of saving his life. He was only stunned
by the blow and soon recovered.

" In the meantime the cattle recognised them and set
up a tremendous bellowing with wonted sounds on
such occasions. This roused the Lochaber men, but
seeing nothing, they were soon lulled into repose.
When all was again quiet, the MacFarlanes advanced,
and the Laird gave the signal of attack by shooting
the sentinel who leapt into the air and fell weltering
in his blood. The attack began on all sides, and the
MacFarlanes soon repulsed the ingrates who barricaded
the door, and thus offered a temporary resistance.
The laird, forgetful of old Marjory's vision, seized a
burning faggot and set fire to the hovel, and the poor

Lochaber men were soon burned to death. The Laird reflected that he might have shown mercy, but it was too late.

" A .violent hurricane arose at the same time, and the flames soon communicated to the adjoining forest. The poor cattle alone burst through the flames and escaped destruction. The MacFarlanes were surrounded on all sides, and were obliged to lie down in a pool of water to preserve themselves from being burnt. They were soon obliged to quit this place of refuge, and were scattered in all directions. The Laird, accompanied by the faithful Angus, pursued their way for some time, till at length the Laird was knocked down by a falling brand and swooned away.

" When he came to himself he saw poor Angus lying under a great tree which had fallen on him. He cut away with his broadsword the intervening trunk and at last succeeded in extricating his lifeless body. The Laird had no time for consideration, but putting the body on his shoulders, bore him away into that mournful solitude. He had not proceeded far when he met the distracted Ellen who on seeing the body of her future husband, fell down and expired at his feet. The Laird hesitated a moment whether he should leave the bodies where they were to be burnt to ashes, or carrying them on his shoulders, expose himself, already sinking from fatigue, to the devouring element which was fast approaching him. He nobly chose the latter, and placing one corpse on each shoulder, trudged on. At length, almost exhausted, he fell in with a party of his followers, who relieved him of his burden, and soon after they reached a place of safety.

" What a mournful gathering was that to behold! Nothing but flames extending as far as the eye could reach. The very deer coming for refuge, and seeking for protection from man.

" Thus was the vision of old Marjory fully and dreadfully realised."

MacFarlane, as we have said, was a faithful follower of the great Montrose, and the Clan formed the vanguard of his forces, which penetrated through the mountains amid snowdrifts to the music of "Thogail nam Bo," and fell upon the army of Argyle at Inverlochy, inflicting upon it a severe defeat, in 1645.

A large number of MacFarlanes seem to have adopted the Grahams of Montrose as their Chief, and to have settled in the parish of Buchanan, in Stirlingshire. In an island of Loch Lomond (Inchcaillioch) there is a joint burying place of the Grahams and MacFarlanes.

That Walter was like his fathers, a prominent Scottish churchman, is shown by the following incident, which speaks for itself.

For marrying Sir John Colquhoun, 16th of Luss, to Margaret Baillie without due proclamation of banns, and other irregularities, Mr. McLauchlan the minister at Luss was deposed from the office of the Holy ministry. This was on 26th December, 1648. On 23rd January, 1649, the Covenant was renewed in the Parish Church of Luss. The following is the extract from the minutes of the Presbytery of Dumbarton :—

"Concerning the vacant church of Luss, and renewing of the Covenant there, Mr. David Elphinstone, Mr. Archd. McLean, and Mr. John Stewart are appointed to repair to the said kirk on Wednesday come eightdays for keeping of the Fast, and the said Mr. David to preach before noon, and Mr. Archd. McLean, afternoon, in the Irish language and betwixt the sermons the said, Mr. David and Mr. John Stewart are to go on, on the trial of the parish, conform to order, and Mr. John Stewart to read the solemn engagement and Covenant after the first sermon, and Mr. Archd. McLean to renew the Covenant on the Sabbath thereafter, and Gillish McArthur, Clerk to the Session, is ordained to have the parishioners duly advised to keep the Fast at the said kirk, and *especially to advise* the Laird of MacFarlane to have his people of the Arrochar present, and the said Mr. David to intimate the vacancy of the place."

The italics are ours.

We regret we have been unable to find any particulars of the campaign of the Commonwealth troops in the Arrochar country, with the twice besieging of Walter in his house, which may have been at Tarbert or the castle on Eilean-a-vow, and the burning of Inveruglas, but certain inferences may be drawn from the following extracts from the Colquhoun chronicles :—

" At the beginning of 1654 Ross Dhu was defended by John Dennistoun of Colgrain (Dennistoun M.S.) who had obtained from Wm. Earl of Glencairn, Commander-in-Chief of the Royalist troops in Scotland, commissions in November and December, 1653. But when Dennistoun marched northward from Rossdhu with the Lennox Fencibles, the castle fell into the hands of a party of Cromwell's soldiers from Glasgow, under the command of Lt.-Col. Cottrell. It was recovered soon afterwards by the royalists, under the command of the Laird of MacNaughton and the eldest son of Sir George Maxwell of Newark. They were again forced to abandon it by a troop of Cromwell's horse under Colonel Cooper.

" In the same year General Middleton, after having been appointed by Charles the Second on the resignation of the Earl of Glencairn, General and Commander-in-Chief of the royalist forces in Scotland, visited Rossdhu when proceeding with the main body of the army, which was then in Sutherland, through the Highlands southward for the purpose of strengthening it by new recruits. His army was refreshed at Ross Dhu and increased in number, but, notwithstanding, he was defeated by Cromwell's troops at Lochnair, on the 26th of July, following. Cromwell's Act of Grace to the people of Scotland was granted in this year."

CHAPTER XVIII.

JOHN—17TH CHIEF.

1664-1679.

Dukes of Lennox.   *Scottish Rulers.*
CHARLES, 5th Duke.   CHARLES II., 1660-1685.
FRANCES, His Duchess.

JOHN married Grizel, daughter of Sir Colin Lamond of that Ilk.   Her mother was Beatrice, a daughter of Lord Semple.   If Sir James Semple, whose daughter was John's mother, and this Lord Semple are the same, then John married his cousin on the distaff side.   The pair had no son, but three daughters, Jean married to John Buchanan of Lenie, in 1666, Giles, whose husband was Alexander M'Millan of Dunmore, in 1667, and Grizel, who married Archibald Buchanan of Torie, in 1673.

On the death of Grizel, John married Anne, a daughter of Campbell of Duntroon, who was the widow of " The Captain of Carrick."   By her also he had three daughters, who all married.

The above dates rather indicate that John lived later than the Battle of Bothwell Bridge (1679). The Clan of MacFarlane formed a detachment of the Duke of Monmouth's army, and it is stated were amongst the first in storming the gateway through which the guards charged.

Sir Walter Scott in " Old Mortality " quotes the incident :—

" The defence made by the Covenanters was so

THE BATTLE OF BOTHWELL BRIDGE.

From the painting by Sam Bough, A.R.S.A. Reproduced from "Old Mortality," in the Melrose Edition of the Waverley Novels, by permission of The Caxton Publishing Co.

protracted, and obstinate, that the royal generals began to fear that it might be successful. While Monmouth threw himself from his horse and rallying the Foot Guards, brought them on to another close and desperate attack, he was warmly seconded by General Thomas Dalziel, who, putting himself at the head of a body of Lennox Highlanders, rushed forward with their tremendous war cry ' Loch Sloy ! ' This was the slogan or war cry of the MacFarlanes, taken from a lake near the head of Loch Lomond, in the centre of their ancient possessions on the western banks of that beautiful inland sea."

As John had no son, he was succeeded by his brother Andrew of Ardess (near Rowardennan). This is the first occasion upon which the succession of Chiefs was other than from father to son over a period of four hundred and fifty years.

The first proposal for Arrochar becoming a separate parish, with its own church and glebe, was made in 1648. This was in the time of Walter, 16th Chief, who made the suggestion, but as John dealt with the matter and signed the engagement, we have included the reference here.

From the great extent of the parish of Luss, it had long been considered desirable that the lands of Arrochar, which were the most northerly part of it, should be separated and formed into a distinct parish. The Presbytery of Dumbarton brought the matter before the Council of Estate in Scotland, and on a petition and recommendation from the Presbytery, by an order dated Holyrood House, 24th December, 1658, appointed Robert Hamilton of Barnes and others to be their Commissioners, to call before them all parties interested in the dismembering of the lands of Arrochar from the parish of Luss, and in the erection of a new church at Tarbet, with a manse and the provision of a glebe for the minister, and if they found a general concurrence, that all parties concerned should

forthwith proceed to the building of a church and
manse and to the providing of a glebe, conformably to
the Act of Parliament. To this proposal Sir John
Colquhoun had always been favourable, and he had
frequently expressed his readiness to concur in the
furtherance of so good a work. To carry out the views
of the Presbytery of Dumbarton and the Government,
he, on 25th January, 1659, subscribed a bond to denude
himself of the sum of 400 merks yearly, payable by the
Laird of MacFarlane for the tithes of his lands of
Arrochar and 15 bolls teind meal, payable forth of the
lands in Arrochar (Stuckgown) belonging to Walter
MacFarlane of Gartartan, in favour of the minister of
Tarbet and his successors in all time coming, and to be
uplifted by the first minister after his entry to the
ministry at Tarbet.

John MacFarlane, fiar of Arrochar, is stated also to
have been favourable to the division of the parish of
Luss, and granted a bond also dated 25th January,
1659, binding himself to cause, begin, finish and perfect
the building of a new kirk with a manse for the
minister of Tarbet, and also to give and mortify a
competent glebe, under the pain of 3,000 merks Scots,
to be uplifted by the Presbytery of Dumbarton and
employed by them for pious uses, within the said lands
of Arrochar, " seriously entreating the said Commissioners and all parties concerned forthwith to
proceed in all points, conform to the said order " of the
Council of Estate in Scotland. From Fraser we take
the following, in this connection :

"Not only was the church (at Luss) inadequate for
the population, but it was extremely inconvenient for
the parishioners in the bounds of Arrochar, in its
northern part, who, from their distance, could not
attend the church, especially during the winter months.
It was therefore felt to be very desirable to form these
lands into a separate parish. In 1648, the matter
was brought under the consideration of the Presbytery

of Dumbarton by MacFarlane, the Laird of Arrochar, who, being the only heritor within the lands to be disjoined, with the exception of MacFarlane of Gartartan, offered to defray the expenses of building a church and manse, and to provide a glebe for the new parish.

"In 1649, the new parish was perambulated by the Presbytery, who selected the site of the church at West Tarbet. But for many years after this nothing practical was done. At the end of the year 1658, the Presbytery laid the case before the Council of Estate in Scotland, who, in compliance with the request of the Presbytery, appointed commissioners to summon before them, and to hear parties interested in the disjunction of the lands of Arrochar from the parish of Luss, and in the erection of a new church at Tarbet, with a manse, and the provision of a glebe for the minister. Favourable to the object proposed, Sir John Colquhoun of Luss, by a bond dated 25th January, 1659, became bound to denude himself of the tithes of the lands of Arrochar, and John MacFarlane, fiar of Arrochar, bound himself, by a bond of the same date, to erect a church and manse, and to provide a competent glebe. But these arrangements were not yet brought to a practical issue. In 1676, another perambulation of the new parish, by the Presbytery of Dumbarton, took place. The following is the minute of Presbytery narrating this perambulation :—

" Presbytery Dumbarton at Tarbet,
September 10, 1678.

" Sederunt—Moderator, Messrs. William Andersone, Arthur Miller, Thomas Allan, James Buchanan, William M'Kechnie.

" The brethren foresaid, having met at Lusse, and travelled al the way from thence to Tarbet, and seen the bounds to the end of Lochlomond, northward, sixteen miles distant from the Kirk of Lusse on the one side, and from Tarbet to the side of Lochlong on the other side, and seen the bounds to the head of Lochlong, lying likewise at a great distance from the Kirk of Lusse, and haveing considered the vastnesse of the distance, as said is, and ruggedness of the way, finde it absolutely necessarie that there be a dismembratione, and a church built at the Tarbet, within the Laird of MacFarlane's land, for the accommodatione of the people of these bounds, that the people from the foot of Glendowglasse, and upward upon the side of Lochlomond, and from Gorton in the paroch of Row, to the head of Lochlonge (informed to be about the number of 400 souls,) may repaire thither to attend the ordinances, who are now living in ignorance."

The Rev. H. S. Winchester, we think, has grasped the human aspect of the matter when he writes :

" The MacFarlanes continued to look upon the erection of a separate parish as a new and unnecessary intrusion, and the building of a new church as a needless expense. Luss was their church, the church of their fathers. True, it was ten miles from Arrochar and situated, now, within the lands of their enemies, but it was near enough and convenient enough for all practical purposes ; for to tell the truth the Mac-Farlanes seemed to have little use for a church except for purposes of burial. And so, while the Presbytery set the ecclesiastical machinery in order, and put in a minister, and while John MacFarlane had perforce to pay the stipend, he paid little heed to his promise to provide a church and manse."

In the year 1679 a threat by the MacDonalds to invade the Western Highlands was apparently to be met by a combined force at the gateway to the Highlands, Tarbet Glen. A number of men were despatched from the territory of Luss, at the expense of Sir James Colquhoun, to the head of Loch Long. This we learn from an account of the intromissions of John Colquhoun, younger, of Camstradden, with the

Laird of Luss's rents of the barony of Luss for that year, which contain the following entries :—

"Item, to allow to the compter his expenses in going with a number of men to the head of Loch Long to protect the country, the time of the MacDonalds, at the Laird's special command, - · - - 040 00 0

"Item, paid to John Colquhoun, officer at the Laird's command for his own and two men's charges at the head of Loch Long, 10 days' time, keeping the country," - · - 010 00 0

As early as 1679 the further encroachment of Colquhoun into the northern Lennox was proceeding, for we find on the 11th of March of that year Sir James Colquhoun, the 18th of Colquhoun and 20th of Luss (it was the marriage of a Colquhoun with "the Heiress of Luss," of the old Lennox stock that brought the Colquhouns from Kilpatrick to Rossdhu), obtained a gift of the ward and non-entries of the lands which belonged to his deceased father, from the Commissioners of Frances, Duchess of Lennox, widow of the late Charles, Duke of Lennox. These included Drumfad, Tullichintaull and Finart, the first two be it noted the former lands of the implacable Dougal MacDouill Vic Neil MacFarlane, whose father was slain by Sir Humphrey Colquhoun.

CHAPTER XIX.

ANDREW—18TH CHIEF.
1679-1685.

Earl of Lennox.   *Scottish Rulers.*
FRANCES, Duchess of Lennox.   CHARLES II., 1660-1685.
                                 JAMES VII., 1685-1688.

ANDREW of Ardess declared his coat-of-arms in 1672 (Heraldry Office, Edinburgh). This was previous to his accession to the Chieftainship of the Clan.

His first wife was Elizabeth, daughter of John Buchanan of Ross and Drumakill, by whom he had two sons, John his heir, and Walter, who died unmarried.

By his second wife, Jean, daughter of Campbell of Strachan, he had five sons, Andrew, William, Duncan, Archibald, and another Walter. Andrew, William, Archibald, and Walter were all officers in the British Army, the first named being a major. He, Archibald, and Walter were all killed in the battle of Malplaquet, September 11th, 1709, in the reign of Queen Anne. William married a daughter of Govan of Buchapel without surviving issue. Duncan, described as a Captain, married a French lady by whom he had two sons, Major James, who married Jean, daughter of Sir Alexander Forbes of Foveran, and Duncan, who went to Jamaica and was alive in 1764. In a letter written by Duncan MacFarlane of Muckroy to his father, Alexander, second son of James the first Laird of Muckroy, from Edinburgh, where Duncan was a merchant, he says, " There is just now in town a cousin of the Laird of MacFarlane, son to Captain

ARMS OF ANDREW OF ARDESS.

REGISTERED, 1672.

Andrew succeeded to Chieftainship of Clan MacFarlane in 1679, and apparently retained his own variation of the Arms; a sword in the right hand of the demi-savage in place of a sheaf of arrows, as in the original device.

Duncan, come from Jamaica. He goes back again in Spring." This letter is dated November 23rd, 1764.

Captain Duncan's issue died out, unless the subject of this letter left a family of which in that case the present male representative would appear to be the chief of MacFarlane. The descendants of Andrew of Ardess are of first importance in any consideration of the lineal descent. As we have stated, Andrew had seven sons. The eldest, John, succeeded his father and his line (the main stem) has died out. Walter, the second son, died young. Major Andrew fell at Malplaquet and did not marry. The fourth son, William, also an officer in the army, married but left no surviving issue. Captain Duncan the fifth son had two sons, Captain James and Duncan, but we do not know, as stated above, whether his son Duncan, who was alive in 1764, left a family. Failing male descendants of Duncan there remains only the two youngest sons of Andrew of Ardess, Archibald and Walter. They also were killed at the battle of Malplaquet. We do not know if either of them married and had children, but we have the fact that Malcolm, the progenitor of the Hunston House family, in Ireland, is claimed to be a nephew of their eldest brother, John, the 19th Chief.

CHAPTER XX.

JOHN—19TH CHIEF.
1685-1705.

Scottish Rulers.

JAMES VII.,   1685-1688.
WILLIAM AND MARY, 1689-1694.
WILLIAM,   1689-1702.
ANNE,   1702-1714.

JOHN was chief for about twenty years. In the reign of James VII. he was in command of 400 of his own men who were ordered to the shire of Renfrew to keep the peace in that county, but disliking the conditions of the times, he soon retired and could never afterwards be prevailed upon to undertake such a mission. With the landing of the Prince of Orange he espoused the cause of William and Mary, so that the clansmen who fought on the side of Claverhouse at Bothwell Bridge were now opposed to the dashing Marquis of Dundee.

When the Convention of the Estates sitting at Edinburgh were alarmed by the news of Dundee being in arms, John (1688) offered to raise a regiment of his own men to assist the Government. The campaign, however, coming to an abrupt close with the death of Claverhouse at the battle of Killiecrankie, the need for MacFarlane's force disappeared. The Chief was afterwards appointed Colonel of a regiment of foot. This would be in 1689 or 1690.

John married twice. His first wife was Agnes, daughter of Sir Hugh Wallace of Woolmot. Their only son, Andrew, died young.

John's second wife was Helen, daughter of Robert, second Viscount Arbuthnot. They had four sons and one daughter, Walter, who succeeded as 20th Chief, Robert, who died young, William, who succeeded as 21st Chief, Alexander, and Catherine who died young.

The youngest son, Alexander, entered trade as a merchant, and settled ultimately in Jamaica. There he acquired a considerable fortune. He left a large estate called Large Island, in Jamaica, to his brothers, and died unmarried, in August, 1755. His position in the island community will be understood when we mention that he was one of the assistant judges and a member of the legislative assembly. He was one of the best mathematicians of the age, and a Fellow of the Royal Society. By his will he left to the University of Glasgow, where he was educated, his valuable apparatus of astronomical instruments; and the Observatory, which was shortly after erected by the University on Dovehill, was, as a tribute of honour to his memory for this benefaction, named the MacFarlane Observatory. His property was inherited by his two brothers, Walter of Arrochar and William, who practised as a physician in Edinburgh.

Robert MacFarlane of Brooklyn, whom we have previously quoted, writes of Alexander :—

"It is a fact that the MacFarlanes were of an astronomical turn of mind, and, indirectly this led to the greatest mechanical invention of modern times. Alexander MacFarlane bequeathed all his instruments to the University of Glasgow, and James Watt was sent for, to repair and fit up these instruments in the MacFarlane Observatory. While thus engaged he invented the improved steam-engine with the separate condenser. Watt was a relative of the MacFarlanes, and in his life, by Muirhead, is the following expression about Alexander MacFarlane, ' He carried out one of the mottoes of his family; the Lord my light; the stars my camp.' "

In 1697 John built himself a new house at Inverioch, near Tarbet (Arrochar village); a portion of this still stands forming the rear portion of the present house, and the commemorative stone retains an honourable place over the portal of the present Arrochar House. This stone bears the date 1697, the figures separated by an engraved Scots thistle. Underneath is carved this inscription :—

"THUGADH A CHLACH SO BHO ARD DORUS AN AITREAMH :
A THOG EOIN, TRIATH NAM PARLANAICH,
AGUS TIGHEARNA AN ARRATHIR,
AIR CULTHAOBH AN TIGHE SO,
ANN SA BHLIADHNA ATA SGRIOBHTE ORRA."

A free translation of this Gaelic is the following :— "This stone was taken from the main entrance of the house built by John, Chief of the MacFarlanes and Laird of Arrochar, in the year inscribed upon it."

The Hunston House MacFarlanes possess a painting of which the old house is the subject.

John died, 13th May, 1705, and during his lifetime apparently he had building enough on his hands without troubling about his obligations in regard to the church and manse for the minister. For there had been a minister ever since 1658, the Rev. Archibald MacLachlan, but he demitted his charge in 1701, on the grounds of "infirmities of body and various secular discouragements," which last consisted in the want of a church, manse and glebe. There was no one pining to succeed the Rev. Archibald MacLachlan in this barren parish. We dip once more into Mr. Winchester's racy narrative for his estimate of the situation :—

"A very interesting sidelight is thrown on these times by the records of the Presbytery of Dumbarton, and of the Synod of Glasgow. In 1702 the people of Arrochar wished to get rid of their minister—the Rev. John MacLachlan. Perhaps they had never taken

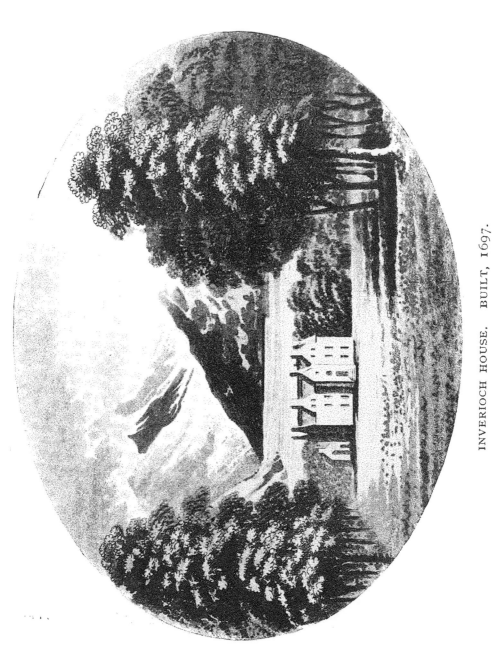

INVERIOCH HOUSE. BUILT, 1697.

Note, this house faces towards Loch Lomond ; Loch Long in background.

kindly to a resident minister, and perhaps the Rev.
John, by his irregular conduct and his neglect of duty,
afforded them some grounds for their discontent; at
anyrate the parishioners brought before the Presbytery
a libel against their minister, and prayed to have him
removed. But the Presbytery of Dumbarton were
not willing to deal harshly with an offending brother,
and so they sought to ease the situation by appointing
an assistant to help him. Now, the assistant whom
they chose for this purpose was one Robert MacFarlane,
one of their own bursars or poor scholars. But
probably Robert knew too much about Arrochar to be
willing to fill the place, and he declined to come. The
Presbytery insisted, and Robert appealed to the
Synod. After considering the whole position, the
Synod determined that Robert MacFarlane must obey
the call of the Presbytery and take up duty in Arrochar,
unless he can prove, as he alleges, ' that there is neither
kirk, nor manse, nor kirk session, nor school in the
parish.'

" Robert proved to the satisfaction of the Synod that
there was none of these things, and while he had to
take up duty in the parish, he was declared to be
' transplantable,' and in due course he was trans-
planted to Fintry (in 1705)."

We read elsewhere that—

" In the MacFarlane burying-ground in the churchyard of Luss is a tombstone over the grave of Mr.
Archd. MacLachlan, the first minister of Arrochar, with
the following inscription :—' Here lies the corpse of
Master Archibald MacLachlan, late Minister of the
Gospel at Tarbet, who departed this life, October,
1731, and of his age 94 years.' "

CHAPTER XXI.

WALTER—20TH CHIEF.

1705-1767.

Scottish Rulers.

ANNE,	1702-1714.
GEORGE I.,	1714-1727.
GEORGE II.,	1727-1760.
GEORGE III.,	1760-1820.

"WALTER MACFARLANE of that Ilk, a man of parts, learning, and knowledge, a most ingenious antiquary, and by far the best genealogist of his time, was possessed," says Sir Robert Douglas, "of the most valuable collection of materials for a work of this kind (genealogical) of any man in the kingdom, which he collected with great judgment, and at a considerable expense, and to which we always had, and still have, free access. This sufficiently appears by the many quotations from MacFarlane's collections both in the Peerage and Baronage of Scotland. In short, he was a man of great benevolence, an agreeable companion, and a sincere friend."

Skene's testimony to the worth of our great antiquary is equally laudatory.

" He is justly celebrated as an indefatigable collector of the ancient records of Scotland. The extensive and valuable collections which his industry has been the means of preserving form the best monument to his memory ; and as long as the existence of the ancient records of the country, or a knowledge of its ancient history remain an object of interest to any Scotsman, the name of MacFarlane will be handed down as one of its benefactors."

In the Preface to " Geographical Collections relating to Scotland," made by Walter MacFarlane, edited from MacFarlane's transcript in the Advocates' Library, Edinburgh, Sir Arthur Mitchell, K.C.B., M.A., M.D., LL.D., writes :—

" It may be an advantage to repeat here the short biographical notices of MacFarlane that Mr. Clark gave in the Genealogical Collections. The first notice of him is taken from ' The Chiefs of Colquhoun and their Country,' Vol. II., pages 99-100, by Sir William Fraser, K.C.B., and is as follows :—

" Walter MacFarlane, one of the most laborious and accurate antiquaries of his age, transcribed with his own hand many old cartularies and muniments deposited in private charter-chests. He was very liberal in allowing access to his valuable collections and transcripts, which are still consulted and often quoted by authors, being regarded as of high authority. To his industry we owe the existence of the Levenax Cartulary, the original of which is now lost. He married Lady Elizabeth Erskine, daughter of Alexander, sixth Earl of Kellie. Little is known of his history, which appears to have been chiefly that of a student, without any remarkable incidents to record. In Anderson's Diplomata Scotæ, published at Edinburgh in the year 1739, the learned editors, Mr. Anderson and Mr. Thomas Ruddiman, in an acknowledgment of their obligations to those who contributed the original charters engraved in that great work, notice in favourable terms the assistance given them by the Laird of MacFarlane, ' In this list of most noble and most eminent men deserves in particular to be inscribed by us a most accomplished young man, Walter MacFarlane of that Ilk, Chief of the MacFarlanes, one of the most ancient of the clans, who, as he is conspicuous for the utmost urbanity, and for his acquaintance with all the most elegant and especially the antiquarian departments of literature, most readily devoted much labour and industry in explaining to us the names of men and places.' The eulogium pronounced upon him by Smollett is elsewhere quoted. He died, without issue, at his town house in the Canongate of Edinburgh, on 5th June, 1767. After his death his valuable collections were purchased by the Faculty of Advocates, Edinburgh. His portrait, an excellent original painting, which exhibits a remarkably intelligent, manly and open countenance, occupies a place on the walls of the Museum of the Society of Antiquaries of Scotland, to whom it was gifted in 1786, by his nephew, Walter MacFarlane. This portrait was engraved by the late Mr. W. B. D. D. Turnbull, for the purpose of being introduced into his ' Monasticon of Scotland,' a work which was never completed."

The next notice is from the Cash Book of the late William MacFarlane of Portsburgh, W.S., who died, 13th July, 1831, and it runs as follows, under date 1785 :—

" He died in his house in the Canongate, Edinburgh, on the 5th, and was buried in the Greyfriars, Edinburgh, betwixt the two west pillars of the New Kirk, on the 8th of June, 1767. He was succeeded by his brother, Dr. William MacFarlane, as 21st of Arrochar, who sold the estate in March, 1784, after having been 559 years in the family."

The Collection of Manuscripts formed by MacFarlane was purchased by the Faculty of Advocates in 1785, from his niece, Miss Janet MacFarlane, for the sum of £21. It consists of :—

1.—The Genealogical Collections, 2 vols., edited by J. T. Clark and published by the Scottish History Society (1900).

2.—The Geographical Collections, 3 vols., edited by Sir Arthur Mitchell and published by the Scottish History Society (1906).

3.—Collections relative to several Scottish Families, 2 vols.

WALTER, 20TH CHIEF OF MACFARLANE.

From a portrait in the possession of the Faculty of Advocates, Edinburgh.

4.—Index to the Register of the Great Seal in 1762, 5 vols.

5.—Diplomatum regiorum quæ in publicis archivis extant Abbreviationes, 10 vols.

6.—Several volumes of transcripts of Charters, including the charters of Melrose, Balmerinoch and other religious houses.

7.—Various other transcripts.

Amongst the yet unpublished MSS. there is a volume described as " Notes of Genealogies of his own Family and the Earls of Lennox " (Advocates MS., 34.3.10).

The reference to Smollett and Walter in the foregoing is as follows :—

" Smollett and his friends, who made a tour into the Western Highlands in the eighteenth century, dined with Walter MacFarlane, then Laird of Arrochar"

In " Humphrey Clinker," the celebrated novelist introduces one of the correspondents in the novel as writing thus :—" I told you, in my last, I had projected an excursion to the Highlands, which project I have now happily executed, under the auspices of Sir George Colquhoun, a colonel in the Dutch Service, who offered himself as our conductor on this occasion. Leaving our women at Cameron, to the care and inspection of Lady H—— C——, we set out on horseback for Inveraray, the county town of Argyle, and dined on the road with the Laird of MacFarlane, the greatest genealogist I ever knew in any country, and perfectly acquainted with all the antiquities of Scotland."

Another correspondent thus writes :—" The poems of Ossian are in every mouth. A famous antiquarian of this country, the Laird of MacFarlane, at whose house we dined a few days ago, can repeat them all in the original gaelic."

While their Chief practised the higher arts, his clan had apparently not reached the same level of advancement. How Rob Roy fared with them in his effort

to raise adherents in the Lennox for the rebellion of
1715, we have no record, but McIan states that in 1745,
the clan mustered 300 men and fought gallantly for
Prince Charlie.

Writing from Winburg, Orange River Colony, David
McFarland writes :—" My family came south with
Prince Charlie and fought with him. One of my
ancestors settled in Lancashire when things had
quietened down."

As we have seen from the last chapter, John, the
19th Chief embraced the cause of the Covenanters and
Whigs, and as Walter's disposition was studious, such
politics as he held were probably of the same colour.
One thing is certain, whatever proportion of the Clan
rallied to the standard of Prince Charlie, they were not
led by their Chief, in person, which probably accounts
for the following reference by Mr. A. M. Mackay in
" The Celtic Monthly "—

" At no time was there one half of the Highland Clans
engaged on the Jacobite side.　From the very beginning
many of them were Covenanters and Whigs—
Campbells, Grants of Strathspey, Colquhouns, Forbeses,
MacFarlanes, MacKays, MacNaughtons, Munros,
Rosses, Sinclairs and Sutherlands.　These were always
on the Hanoverian side, and in the 1745 rising, there
falls to be added the MacDonalds, and MacLeods of
Skye, and the Mackenzies of Seaforth and Kintail, who
were influenced by President Forbes.

Let us put it into figures and we can see how the
matter stood.

The Campbells could put into the field say, 2,000 ;
Colquhouns, 500 ; Forbeses, 500 ; Grants of Strathspey,
600 ;　Mackays, 1,000 ;　MacFarlanes, 300 ;　Mac-
Naughtons, 300 ;　Munros, Rosses, 600 ;　Sinclairs,
1,000 ; The Earl of Sutherland, 1,500.　To which we
add, MacDonalds of Skye and North Uist, 1,000 ;
MacLeods of Skye and Harris, 1,000 ; MacKenzies,
1,500 ; Total, 12,300.

But where, ah where the Campbells' martial crest ?
Where MacKenzie, Munro and all the rest ?
Have Forbes, MacKay and Sutherland no place
Among the chivalry of Albyn's race ?
Where Ross, Sinclair ?   Where Gunn and bold MacRae ?
Where the MacNaughton and the MacLeod array ?
Colquhoun, Buchanan, and MacFarlan too—
Why were their blades lost to the bonnets blue ?

So here we have a direct conflict of evidence. McIan says that three hundred of the clan were " out," while MacKay says the clan did not take part in the rebellion, and that its muster was the same figure—three hundred. Of course it must be remembered that there were by this time many other groups of MacFarlanes besides the men of Arrochar.

Dr. Johnson visited Arrochar in his prejudiced peregrinations through the Highlands. It was Walter who administered the recorded reproof. On meeting, the Doctor said, " How do you do, Mr. MacFarlane ? " whereupon the Chief drew himself up and replied with dignity, " There are many MacFarlanes—I am MacFarlane."

Walter declared his arms at the Court of the Lord Lyon in 1750.

We have been at pains to endeavour to locate the town house in Edinburgh where Walter died, and for help in this matter we have to express our indebtedness to Mr. Will Cowan of 47 Braid Avenue, Edinburgh, who writes :—

" The following is all the information I have been able to obtain regarding the house in the Canongate where Walter MacFarlane lived and died. The Edinburgh Directories contain the following—

1773.—McFarlane of McFarlane, near Queensberry House.

1774-5-6.—William McFarlane of McFarlane, Reid's Close, Canongate.

As Reid's Close is quite near to Queensberry House,

the entry in 1773 no doubt refers to the same address, viz., Reid's Close. The 1773 issue is the earliest Edinburgh Directory. Two points remain doubtful (1) Was MacFarlane's house the one in the main street of the Canongate, at the head or entrance of Reid's Close or was it behind in the Close itself. In those days a house at the head of a Close was often considered as being part of the Close and indeed generally was entered from the Close. In this case the house in that portion is still (1917) standing, and is rather a notable old mansion.

" In Wilson's " Memorials of Edinburgh,' 1848 edition, in Volume II., page 79, there is a front view of the house and in Volume I., page 217, a back view, from the interior of the Close. I have found no reference in any books on Edinburgh to the MacFarlane family in connection with this house. (2) One cannot be certain from the Directory entries, or indeed from the notice of Walter MacFarlane's death, whether he was owner or merely tenant. The lawyers who at present have the title deeds of the property at Reid's Close, say that the older deeds have been lost, and the present existing titles do not go far enough back to settle the question as to whether any MacFarlane ever owned the property."

Resuming the chequered narrative of the parish and its church, we find that in 1709 the Presbytery of Dumbarton obtained a decree of the Court of Session for a church, manse and glebe for the parish of Arrochar, but the carrying out of that decree was delayed, in consequence of the minority of the Laird of MacFarlane (Walter) and of his embarrassed circumstances. Mr. Alexander Graham of Duchray, writing in 1724, says : " In this parish " (Tarbet, now Arrochar) " there is no church yet built." He adds, " all the inhabitants use the Irish language." It was not till 1733 that the church was actually built. The manse was built in 1837.

COMMUNION CUPS,

Presented to Arrochar Church, by Hon. Helen Arbuthnot, wife of Walter, 20th Chief; still in service.

Some of the ruins of the old church of Arrochar remain. Above the principal door, which has been preserved, the date of 1733 is carved in very beautiful figures. This may be held as the year in which the church was completed, and it shows the great delay of nearly a century in building it after negotiations for the separation of Arrochar as a parish from the parish of Luss had commenced. The present church was built in 1847.

In 1742, the Honourable Helen Arbuthnot, daughter of Robert, Second Viscount Arbuthnot, second wife of John MacFarlane, the 19th Chief, afterwards wife of Mr. John Spotswoode of that Ilk, made a present of Communion Cups for the Church of Arrochar. On the cups is engraved the crest of the Arbuthnot family, being a peacock's head on a wreath, couped proper, with the following inscription :—" The gift of the Honourable Helen Arbuthnot to the Parish of Arroquhar." There is no date on the cups. This lady also bequeathed the sum of two hundred merks Scots to purchase a bell for the kirk of Arrochar, and also five hundred merks Scots for behoof of the poor of the parish. Her son Walter, granted an obligation, dated at New Tarbet, 3rd September, 1745, to the minister and other members of the Kirk-Session of Arrochar, for the 200 merks above mentioned, with the interest thereof from the term of Whitsunday, 1742, and he also granted bills to the minister and Kirk-Session for the payment of the other sum. But neither of these legacies was paid to the Kirk-Session for many years after. Walter the son of the donor, having died in 1767, the estates of William, his brother, who succeeded him, and John, William's son, were then vested in trustees on behalf of their creditors. The estates of Arrochar were sold in the year 1785. It was not, however, till the year 1802 that the Kirk-Session received complete payment of the two hundred merks bequeathed by Helen Arbuthnot, the Lady of Arrochar, the seventh and last dividend due to the Kirk-Session out of the estates of the then deceased William and John MacFarlane being then paid. The Session now resolved to apply this money to the purpose for which it was originally bequeathed. Delays, however, again occurred. Thirteen years elapsed before the bell was actually acquired. At the Kirk-Session of Arrochar, 3rd January, 1815, Mr. Gillespie, minister of the parish, reported that he had bought a bell for the church from Mr. Brownlee of Greenock, in October, 1813, which amounted to £24 3s. 10d.; Lady Helen Arbuthnot having left money for the purpose. The bell amounted to the above sum, including freight, chain, rope, the smith's and wright's accounts, and other incidental expenses.

"The bell was bought," writes Mr. Winchester, "sixty years after the legacy for its purchase was left, and hung in a tree—known to this day as the bell tree —for there was no place for a bell in the plain structure of the old kirk; and when the new church was built in 1847, the bell was taken down from its place in the bell tree and placed where it now hangs in the church tower.

"While the bell hung in the bell tree it was a source of great temptation to ill disposed persons to take a pull at the rope, and an old inhabitant relates the following story of such an abuse :—

"Malcolm MacFarlane, an erring parishioner, had been summoned to a Kirk Session in the manse in a case of discipline. Malcolm had been rather faithfully handled by the court, and he left the manse in an angry mood. On his way home he passed the bell tree, and it occurred to him that he might take a pull at the bell just to relieve his feelings. But just at that moment a neighbour's goat wandered past, and Malcolm seized him and securing the bell rope to his horns, withdrew to a safe place to watch what would happen. Of course the goat tugged and struggled to escape, and the bell rang with irregular and broken sounds, and out came minister and session to see what the cause of the strange noises might be. Seeing an uncanny looking thing with horns rushing to and fro in the faint light, and tugging furiously at the bell rope, some of the Session thought it must be the devil himself, and it was only when the minister mustered up courage enough to approach the tree that he found the fiend to be nothing more than old Mary Campbell's goat."

One of the ministers of the parish during Walter's period was the Rev. Alexander MacFarlane, who died in 1763. He was a distinguished Gaelic scholar, and a great wit. He is credited with having lampooned his Chief, Walter, in Gaelic verse because, after 1746, he introduced south country farmers and their customs into the clan country. The lines appear as a note to a poem " MacFarlan's Lament," in a volume by James MacGregor, Edinburgh, under the title of " Albyn's Vale and other poems." The publishers were—Edinburgh, A. Constable & Co. and Oliver & Boyd ; London, Longman & Co., 1824. Apparently it is impossible to translate the lines satisfactorily into English, as the feature of the poem is a play upon the words embodied in it, but for the benefit of our Gaelic speaking readers we quote the lines :—

Tha Factor aig MacPharlain is tha mi mealltach
Mur ann de Shliochd a' Ghearrain,
Thug e thugainn Calcadair an aodaich
Is slaodar de thrusdair Sionnaich
Dcchas a' choilich Fhrangaich, Ian do
Shamhuinn le dha gheal-shuil.
Naile ! chunnaic mi cailleach le cuigeal
A chuireadh a' chuideachd ud thairis air Leamhuinn.

CHAPTER XXII.

WILLIAM—21ST CHIEF.
1767-1787.

Scottish Rulers.
GEORGE III., 1760-1820.

DR. WILLIAM succeeded his brother as 21st Chief and, as events were to prove, he was the last MacFarlane to hold sway at Arrochar. No more " the power of pit and gallows," no more leading of wild Highlandmen to the stirring shout of " Loch Sloy," no more levying of the Earl's blackmail and the defence of the same against harriers from the North. The glory had departed. The leaven of modern civilisation had bitten deep into the heart of MacFarlane, and the old race was outworn. It could not bear transplanting, and presently died out.

William was a physician, and practised in Edinburgh, so we expect the clan was left pretty much to its own resources. The district, nevertheless, remained almost exclusively MacFarlane, for as late as 1804 the old ledger of the Tarbet store contains scarcely any other name. That there was little or no affinity between the clansmen and the Chief, and, we may add, their minister, is shown by the following extract from " The Old Statistical Account of Scotland," written by that clergyman in 1790 :—" The people of this parish are mostly MacFarlane, and until lately, they have always had a strong attachment to the Laird as Chief ; and while this subsisted, misanthropy and ferocity were marked features in their character."

The writer was the Rev. John Gillespie—a very different type of clergyman to that one who went tearing through the heather and bracken, sword in hand, after the Suinert men, or even the kindly parsons who went out of their way to warn the illicit whisky distillers of their flock, when the gaugers were around.

William married Christian, daughter of James Dewar of Vogrie. They had a numerous family, of whom three sons and three daughters survived childhood—John, Walter, Robert, Janet, Helen and Rachel.

In our Introductory chapter we stated that Mac-Farlane's banshee was a black goose, and true to the record of all ancient families, the fate of MacFarlane was predicted. The story runs as follows :—

" In the time of the last Chief of the Clan MacFarlane, who was Laird of Arrochar, there was a man named Robert MacPharic, who lived at Inverioch, and who pretended to be possessed of the gift of ' second sight ' ; he was at one time, with some others, on Stronafine Hill, and slept. He awakened suddenly, and said : ' MacFarlane's time at Arrochar will not be long, and the person who comes in his place will be a stranger to us, and will make parlour and kitchen a pig-sty ; and shortly before that happens, a black goose will come and remain among MacFarlane's geese. It will not be known where the goose came from, nor whither it went.' He also said : ' There will be four bridges where there is now but one, on the estate. MacFarlane will shortly after leave Arrochar, and his clan will lose all trace of him.' One day, soon after this, a black goose alighted among MacFarlane's geese as they were feeding, and after eating, flew into a tree. No one cared to interfere with it ; it remained, feeding with the geese, and stayed nights in the tree for about three months, and then disappeared."

Mrs. MacFarlane Little contends that the prophecy was thus fulfilled :—

" Shortly after this, war broke out between America

and Great Britain. MacFarlane was heavily taxed, and was also deeply in debt.

" His family had been reared in luxury. Gambling with cards was then considered respectable. He entertained with a more princely hospitality than the revenues of the estate could support. He sold an estate that he owned in Jamaica (probably the legacy of his brother Alexander.—*Ed.*) for £8,000, but could not avert the threatened ruin, and in 1784, the Barony of Arrochar, which for six hundred years had been in the possession of the MacFarlanes, passed into the hands of strangers.

" A Mr. Douglas was appointed factor for Ferguson, and lived in ' the old castle.' An old man of Arrochar told the writer that he had seen the kitchen used as a pig-sty, and a well-known clergyman had seen ' a lot of Shetland ponies stabled in the keep of the castle.'

" The Duke of Argyll, wishing to make a new road to his Castle of Inveraray, built three new bridges on the estate of Arrochar.

" So all of MacPharic's prophecies came true."

The Rev. H. S. Winchester has it that MacPharic said specifically that the four bridges would cross Ault Phollaig (the small burn at Arrochar House), and points out that the fourth bridge was built over this stream when the Duke of Argyll made his new road along Loch Longside to Roseneath. Also he mentions that the keep of the castle was actually used as a stable when the front had been rebuilt and was being used as an hotel in the beginning of the nineteenth century.

Investments in the Darien scheme apparently put the copestone upon William's ruin. An important creditor, or an agent for creditors, was a certain Hugh Mossman, a writer of Edinburgh. In 1784, the estate was brought to a judicial sale. The following is the Memorial and Abstract of Process of Sale, from *The Stirling Antiquary* :—

MEMORIAL AND ABSTRACT OF PROCESS OF SALE OF MACFARLANE OF MACFARLANE'S ESTATES, 7TH JULY, 1784.

At the instance ot

HUGH NORMAN, eldest son and heir served and returned to the deceased Hugh Mossman, writer in Edinburgh

Agt.

William Macfarlane, Esq. of Macfarlane, John Macfarlane, Junior thereot, and their creditors.

Rental of the lands and Barony of Arrochar and others in the Shire of Dumbarton.

DOWN.—The half of the lands of Down—Malcolm Macfarlane and his mother lease 21 years from Whitsunday, 1766, money rent, £10 13s.

DOWN.—The other half of Down; Peter and Donald Macintyre, 19 years, 1768.

ARDLEISH.—Ardleish; Dougal and Alexander Macdougals, now Malcolm Macfarlane, a stone ot butter at the proven conversion of 10s. is added to the money rent—19 years.

BLAIRSTANG AND STUCKMUD.—Malcolm Macfarlane and Margaret Campbell.

GARVUAL, Margaret Lauder. After Whit., 1787, the rent rises to £42.

GARRACHIE AND ARDLUIE.—Alexander Macfarlane Shicandroin.

UPPER ARDVORLICH.

UPPER INVEROUGLASS and forest of BEINVEURLIC and NETHER ARDVOURLIC.

CAENMORE and BLAIREUNICH.

Part of TARBET called INVERCHULIN.

HILL OF TARBET.

Part of TARBET called CLADDOCHBEG.

CLADDOCH mire with the laigh park of Balhenaan.

COINLACH.

TYUNLOAN.

Part of TARBET.

Another part of ditto.

EASTER BALHENNAN.

Pendicle of BALHENNAN and House and Wynd at TY VICHATTAN.

Part of Balhennan.

STUCKNACLOICH.

UPPER AND NETHER STUCKINTIBBERT.

FIRKEN.

Mill of CAMBUSNACLACH and Mill Lands.

NETHER INVEROUGLASS.

CHOILCORRAN and INVERGROIN, GARTANFAIRED and GREITNEIN, expiration of present lease £88 4s. 9½d.

TYNALARACH ARDINNY and MUIRLAGAN.

STRONFYNE GLENLUYNS and the lands and mill of PORTCHIRBLE and hill of BEINVEIN.

TYNACLACH.

The Baron Officers sons pay for attune.

TULLICHENTAAL.

The tenant pays over and above his rent the stipend to the minister of Luss, being 3 bolls meal, 8½ stone to the boll, and 40s. Scots, or 3s. 4d. of money and 3s. 1d. for Communion elements, and as the payment of stipend agrees with the teind duty in the feu charter to the superior, it is not here added to their rental nor is it hereafter stated as a deduction. The school salary being 4s. 3d., is also paid by the tenant over and above the rent. Stuckgown comprehending Stuckdon and Stuckvolge—George Syme, vassal, John Brock in Garshuke, and Archibald Maclachan, tacksman in Bunnackrae, both bred farmers and grassers concur in deponing that they both together visited and inspected the farms of Inveresk and Balfrone and parks about the mansion house of New Tarbet, all in the natural possession of Macfarlane, and that in their opinion they were worth upon a 19 years' lease of yearly rent £47 10s. 0d.

Money Rent £ s. d.	Hens	Chickens	Doz. of Eggs	Wedders	Loads of Peats	Days of a Man and Horse	Days of a Man
10 13 0	1	10	10	—	—	6	—
10 13 0	2	10	10	—	—	6	—
43 5 0	—	—	—	—	—	—	—
24 0 0	—	—	—	—	—	6	—
26 11 6	—	—	—	—	—	—	—
30 0 0	—	—	—	3	—	—	—
27 10 6	1	12	12	—	—	12	—
14 13 0	2	10	10	—	—	6	—
79 17 9	—	—	—	—	—	—	—
23 3 0	2	—	—	—	—	—	—
4 16 4	1	6	6	—	—	—	6
9 7 $7\frac{7}{12}$	2	6	6	—	12	6	—
6 9 $9\frac{4}{12}$	2	6	6	—	12	—	8
20 19 $11\frac{1}{2}$	3	6	6	—	—	6	—
6 4 $2\frac{2}{12}$	—	—	—	—	—	—	—
3 2 6	1	6	6	—	4	4	—
2 0 0	1	3	3	—	—	—	—
0 15 0	1	—	—	—	—	—	—
10 3 $10\frac{4}{12}$	2	6	6	—	—	6	—
9 4 0	2	6	6	—	—	—	6
3 15 0	2	—	—	—	—	—	—
3 0 0	1	—	—	—	—	—	—
11 13 $2\frac{1}{2}$	4	12	12	—	—	—	12
12 13 0	4	12	12	—	—	6	—
5 5 $6\frac{8}{12}$	—	—	—	—	—	10	—
4 4 8	—	—	—	—	—	2	—
17 19 $10\frac{4}{12}$	—	—	—	—	—	10	—
47 7 7	—	—	—	—	—	—	—
53 15 6	—	—	—	—	—	—	—
65 19 $2\frac{9}{12}$	—	—	—	—	—	—	—
6 10 0	—	—	—	—	—	—	—
1 10 0	—	—	—	—	—	—	—
32 0 0	2	—	—	—	—	—	—
0 10 0	—	—	—	—	—	—	—
47 10 0	—	—	—	—	—	—	—
677 3 $7\frac{2}{12}$	36	111	111	3	28	86	32

Carried forward, £677 3 $7\frac{2}{12}$

K

		£	s	d
Brought forward,		£677	3	$7\frac{2}{12}$
36 Hens at 8d. each,	... ...	1	4	0
111 Chickens at 4d. each,	... ...	1	17	0
111 doz. Eggs at 3d. per doz.,	... ...	1	7	9
3 Wedders, 10s. each,	... ...	1	10	0
28 Loads Peats, 6d. per Load,	... ...	0	14	0
		£683	16	$4\frac{2}{12}$

Tenants pay cess above Rent, total valued
    Rent of the above lands, £738 3s. 4d.,
    after deduction of lands feued to George
    Syme.

Total cess of these lands,	... ...	13	3	$3\frac{4}{12}$
		£696	17	$7\frac{6}{12}$
Deduction, ...	... ...	34	14	$2\frac{7}{12}$
Free Rent,	... ...	662	5	$4\frac{11}{12}$

Abstract of the different proven values—
    1st.—The lands and barony of Arrochar
        and others in the Shire of Dum-
        bartonshire, 25 years purchase of
        free rent and value of woods £3,200,

		19,756	15	$2\frac{11}{12}$

    2nd.—Lands of Burnhouses in the shire of
        Berwick, 22 years purchase, ...

		1,501	10	0

    3rd.—The lands of Bartlaws and Hunt-
        field, in the Shire of Lanark, 22
        years' purchase of free proven
        rental, 5 years' purchase of land
        (£38 13s. 4d.), ...

		1,604	18	$10\frac{8}{12}$
Debts		£22,863	4	$1\frac{7}{12}$

Due and noted, £42,918 2s. $4\frac{8}{12}$d.
Lands in Dumbarton, deductions.
Tullichintane held of Sir James Colquhoun
    of Luss feu, ...

		0	11	$1\frac{4}{12}$

At entry 20 merks, every successor 40 merks.
Stipend to minister of—

Arrochar out of these lands,	£28	17	$9\frac{6}{12}$
Schoolmaster of Arrochar,	5	5	$3\frac{9}{12}$

		34	3	$1\frac{3}{12}$

Tiends of Macfarlane's Arrochar, 80 merks
    Scots.

Tiends of Nether Arrochar 12 merks, or	...	0	13	4
12 Bolls Meal, at 10s. per Boll,	... ...	6	0	0
		£6	13	4

Considerably below stipend,

Macfarlane's Arrochar, 400 merks,	...	22	4	$5\frac{4}{12}$
Nether Arrochar,	... ...	6	13	4
		£28	17	$9\frac{4}{12}$

GLASGOW.   A. C.

The estates were purchased by Ferguson of Wraith for £28,000, who in 1821 sold them to Sir James Colquhoun, Bart., of Luss, for £78,000.

William frequently visited a Parlane MacFarlane in Glasgow, who was one of the largest merchants of that city, conducting a considerable foreign trade. The Chief was wont to arrive in a handsome coach drawn by four fine horses, and on these occasions all Saltmarket turned out to see him pass. Upon one of these visits the chief requested Parlane to send abroad for a china tea service for him. A design was accordingly drawn, and in due course the tea service arrived, decorated with the chief of MacFarlane's arms, along with a duplicate set which, it is said, the Laird had quietly ordered for a gift to Parlane. What was Parlane's relationship to William is unknown, but Parlane's son, also named Parlane, in 1822, visited in Edinburgh two daughters of the Arrochar house, who were in receipt of a Government pension. On his taking his leave, wishing to give him some memento of his visit, the ladies presented Parlane with a delicate and quaint china tea-cup and saucer, which is still preserved by the son of Parlane's second son, David, also named Parlane, who is a merchant in Glasgow. Other descendants of Parlane possess two china plates, which bear the arms of a Chief of MacFarlane, and are doubtless the remains of the duplicate presentation set referred to above. The ladies of the Arrochar family were doubtless Janet, William's eldest daughter, and Margaret, daughter of William's eldest son, John, as it is known that they lived together in Edinburgh. William died in 1787.

A picture of High Street, Glasgow, showing the elder Parlane's premises with his name over the door, was exhibited at a recent Glasgow Exhibition, lent by Mr. W. Kirsop. Parlane the younger, was buried in the Ramshorn Churchyard, Glasgow.

The estates were purchased by Ferguson of Wraith for £28,000, who in 1821 sold them to Sir James Colquhoun, Bart., of Luss, for £78,000.

William frequently visited a Parlane MacFarlane in Glasgow, who was one of the largest merchants of that city, conducting a considerable foreign trade. The Chief was wont to arrive in a handsome coach drawn by four fine horses, and on these occasions all Saltmarket turned out to see him pass. Upon one of these visits the chief requested Parlane to send abroad for a china tea service for him. A design was accordingly drawn, and in due course the tea service arrived, decorated with the chief of MacFarlane's arms, along with a duplicate set which, it is said, the Laird had quietly ordered for a gift to Parlane. What was Parlane's relationship to William is unknown, but Parlane's son, also named Parlane, in 1822, visited in Edinburgh two daughters of the Arrochar house, who were in receipt of a Government pension. On his taking his leave, wishing to give him some memento of his visit, the ladies presented Parlane with a delicate and quaint china tea-cup and saucer, which is still preserved by the son of Parlane's second son, David, also named Parlane, who is a merchant in Glasgow. Other descendants of Parlane possess two china plates, which bear the arms of a Chief of MacFarlane, and are doubtless the remains of the duplicate presentation set referred to above. The ladies of the Arrochar family were doubtless Janet, William's eldest daughter, and Margaret, daughter of William's eldest son, John, as it is known that they lived together in Edinburgh. William died in 1787.

A picture of High Street, Glasgow, showing the elder Parlane's premises with his name over the door, was exhibited at a recent Glasgow Exhibition, lent by Mr. W. Kirsop. Parlane the younger, was buried in the Ramshorn Churchyard, Glasgow.

The following table shows Parlane's descendants :—

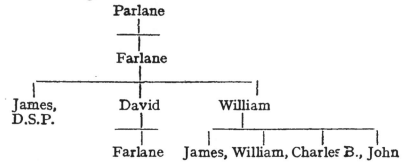

```
                        Parlane
                           |
                    _____|_____
                           |
                        Farlane
                           |
         _____|_____
         |                 |                 |
      James,            David            William
      D.S.P.              |                 |
                     _____|_____      _____|_____
                     |         |      |       |        |          |
                  Farlane   James, William, Charles B., John
```

Charles B. MacFarlane is the eminent amateur golfer and he took part in founding the English section of the Society of the Clan.

Of the laird's children John, the eldest son succeeded his father as 22nd Chief of the Clan, although no longer of the Barony of Arrochar. Of him later.

The next brother Walter, married Marion, only child of John Trotter of Morton Hall, and they had five children, William (born 1769), Christian (born 1770), Janet (born 1774), Alexander Trotter (born 1779), and Robert (born 1780). The first four all appear in order in the Parochial Register of the County of Edinburgh. During that period the family resided at Saughton Hall, but when Robert, the youngest child was born they were living at Fountain Bridge, Edinburgh. William, the eldest son, went to sea and was first mate on an East Indiaman, under the command of the Hon. Captain Elphinstone. He died, unmarried, at St. Helena, before 1811. Of the daughters, we only know that two of them were trained to be milliners in Edinburgh, and afterwards followed the same business in London. One of them is said to have married a Mr. Loch. Of the second son, Alexander Trotter MacFarlane we have no information, but of the youngest son, Robert, Miss Jean MacFarlane Scott, writes : " I could not trace his birth register in any of the church or parish records although I searched very carefully, giving time and close attention. I knew he was grandson of William MacFarlane of MacFarlane (21st Chief) and cousin to my own great-great-grand-father (William, son of John, 22nd Chief), and in putting all together that I knew and could find out, I felt sure he was the third son of Walter MacFarlane and Marion Trotter. Robert was born 1780, married 1815, and died in 1843. He left two sons and a daughter. The eldest son died ten years later and the daughter soon after. The youngest son, Henry, was in the army and went to India. There he had a sunstroke which affected his mind so much that he was in a private asylum from 1839 to 1892, when he died. None of the children married. Robert was often with his cousin Francis, whose grand-father Malcolm founded the Irish branch."

Walter, Robert's father, was alive in 1794, as in that year he presented the portrait of his uncle, Walter (the 21st Chief) to the Antiquary Society of Scotland.

Of the third son of William, Robert, our information is meagre and conjectural. He married, and had three daughters, one of whom died unmarried. The other two, unmarried, were living in Edinburgh in 1816. Robert is stated to have held a sinecure office and lived at Brompton, London, and is believed to be the same with the miscellaneous writer, Robert MacFarlane, M.A., who was killed, being run over by a carriage in Hammersmith, on 8th August, 1804; but another account states that he was alive in 1827.

Of William's three daughters, we have only an account of Janet, the eldest. As we have mentioned she lived with her niece in Edinburgh, where they were visited by Parlane of Glasgow. "The last survivor of the family of William MacFarlane of Arrochar," writes Fraser, "was Miss Janet, or, as she was generally called, Jess MacFarlane, who became the lineal representative of the MacFarlanes of Arrochar. She was a frequent visitor at Rossdhu. Being quite a character in her way . . . . . she was generally called

'The Chief.' She died on the 2nd December, 1821, and was interred in Greyfriars' Churchyard, Edinburgh."

During William's time, in 1774, the scholarly Dr. Stuart was minister of the parish, and among his many great attainments was a knowledge of the "black art." One day, then, as the learned doctor was walking home from a visit to a parishioner who lived up Loch Lomond-side, he met two "gaugers" just at the foot of the brae on the old Wade Road, near where the public school now stands. Now the reverend doctor had just left his parishioner in the act of preparing some malt for the brew, and he had a shrewd suspicion that the gaugers also knew something of what was going forward, and that they were on their way to catch the smuggler in the act. So, looking the men of the law in the face for some time, the doctor placed his staff across the road at their feet, and after making certain mysterious signs, he directed them to stand where they were until he came back. He then hurried back and warned his parish-ioner, who immediately cleared the coast of all questionable gear, while the poor gaugers stood power-less in the middle of the road until the minister came back and released them.

Several tales go to show that the ministers of Arrochar had a kindly feeling towards the "water of life," and, writes Mr. H. S. Winchester, an amiable toleration of smugglers.

During the middle of the 19th century there were several excisemen stationed in the parish, but in former times the visit of the "gauger" was a regular event, and on two occasions at least the parish minister assisted to defeat the law.

Lawless in other respects, it was not to be expected that the men of Arrochar should have much respect for the excise laws. Nor indeed had they. Shebeens abounded even within living memory. On the road between Tarbet and the Big Rest in Glencroe, the sites of eight places where whisky was sold are still pointed out. There was one at Tarbet, one at Tighvechtan, three in the village of Arrochar, one at the " Highland-man's Height " near the present torpedo station, one at the school house in Glencroe, and one at the Big Rest.

All that now remains of the tavern at the Highland-man's Height is the green slope which was once the garden, and faint traces of the house walls buried in the grass and the heather. Yét the house existed well into the nineteenth century ; and it is believed to have sheltered Robert Burns for a night as he passed this way on his tour to the west. It is said that there exists a letter written by Burns during that journey, and dated from " Knockeribus, Arrochar," There is no place of that name now in Arrochar or the neigh-bourhood, but possibly this was the former name of the Highlandman's Height.

But one parish minister of the time—the Rev. John Gillespie—does not seem to have shared any such sentiments. Writing in the old Statistical Account (1790) he tells that the attachment of the MacFarlanes to their Chief was the main cause of the misanthropy and ferocity of manners which marked their character. But the sale of the estates, the departure of the old Chiefs, the making of the military roads, the settlements of grazers from the low country—all these causes have, in the opinion of that parish minister, " contributed to extinguish the remains of that system of barbarity which so long retarded the civilisation of Europe." And he goes on to say :—" The people are now well-bred, honest, and industrious, and not addicted to the immoderate use of spirituous liquors." As to the use of spirituous liquors, we are staggered to think of the former state of the parish, when we remember that at the time when the reverend gentleman wrote his account, there was a shebeen in almost every corner, and at least six recognised public houses existed between Tarbet and the head of Glencroe.

CHAPTER XXIII.

JOHN—22ND CHIEF.
1787-   .

Scottish Rulers.
GEORGE III., 1760-1820.

JOHN, the first of the landless Lairds, married Catherine, daughter of James Walkinshaw of that Ilk. They had two sons and two daughters, William, James, Margaret Elizabeth, and Christian.

It is persistently stated by writers and historians that William's eldest son and heir " emigrated to America."

This vague statement, coupled with the legal language of the " Memorial and Abstract of Process of Sale of MacFarlane of MacFarlane's Estates," already quoted, caused Mrs. MacFarlane Little in her " Clan Farlan," to conceive an amazing fable. She fell into the extraordinary error of regarding " Hugh Norman, eldest son and heir, served and returned to the deceased Hugh Mossman," as the eldest son and heir of " William MacFarlane, Esq., of MacFarlane." Because of the " Junior " attached to his name, she apparently regarded John as a younger son of William.

The story, based on these flimsy premises, has obtained wide credence in America, where Mrs. Little's book was published, so it is necessary for us to state, clearly and categorically, that Hugh Norman was the son of an Edinburgh writer, named Hugh Mossman, and that John MacFarlane was the eldest son and heir of William MacFarlane of Arrochar.

William, John's eldest son was born 29th May, 1770, and James was born within half an hour of his elder.

PAGES FROM ARROCHAR PARISH REGISTER.

Showing MacFarlane's debts to the Church of Scotland, discharged.

brother. In the record of the birth and baptism of
these children they are said to be the sons of John
MacFarlane, younger of MacFarlane, and Mistress
Catherine Walkinshaw, his spouse, residing at Hermiston,
in the parish of Salton (Arrochar Parish Register, H.M.
General Register House, Edinburgh). To Miss Jean
MacFarlane Scott we owe the following particulars of
the continuance of the parent stem to its extinction,
with her uncle William.

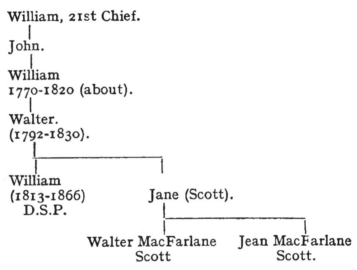

William, 21st Chief.

John.

William
1770-1820 (about).

Walter.
(1792-1830).

William
(1813-1866)   Jane (Scott).
D.S.P.

Walter MacFarlane   Jean MacFarlane
Scott   Scott.

Miss MacFarlane Scott writes, " My mother's brother
was so like Walter, the Antiquary, that if the oil painting
we have of him was placed alongside the one in the
gallery in Edinburgh, you would say, father and son"
    Of Miss Jean MacFarlan Scott herself, we are glad
to reproduce the following tribute, written by the late
Robert MacFarlan of Dumbarton (the rescuer of the
Clan Pibroch), which appeared in *The Celtic Monthly*.
    " With the best blood of two Clans running in her
veins Miss Jean MacFarlan Scott of Sunderland, and
Farmfield, Ayrshire, deserves honourable notice.
Claiming, as she does, to be descended from " Chief
William," the last of the MacFarlanes who held the
ancestral estates of Arrochar, Miss MacFarlan Scott

is no counterfeit or imitation clanswoman.   One cannot
meet her and remain in suspense or uncertainty as to
her being a true clanswoman, jealous for the honour of
Siol nam Parlanach.   This lady of the Clan is not a
voice merely, for the lively force of her mind, united
with good sound sense and business capacity, impel
her to action.   Take an illustration !   The inscription
slab in Greyfriars, Edinburgh, to the memory of Miss
MacFarlane of that ilk, fell out of its place and was
lying unheeded for years, when a private soldier named
MacFarlan tried to fix it up again, but failed.   The
subject of our notice on learning of the circumstance,
had the work done at her own cost and under her own
eye.

" In her search for folklore of her Clan, Miss MacFarlan
Scott has been untiring.   She has spent days in the
Register House, Edinburgh, in Glasgow, and in Luss,
Arrochar, Dumbarton, and numerous other places, in
pursuit of her favourite hobby, and has been in corres-
pondence with MacFarlanes the world over.

" But no notice of Miss MacFarlane Scott would be
complete without making pointed reference to the
marked business ability which she possesses, and which
she has turned to good account.   When her father,
who carried on business in Sunderland, died, she was
thrown upon her own resources, and she has lived to
negative two erroneous but common impressions, that
a woman cannot have business aptitude of a high order,
and that the Celtic craving for folklore, pedigree and the
like is inconsistent with success in the matter of fact
battle of life.   The high-class character of the firm of
Scott & Co., Lorne House, Sunderland, is well known.
It is not so widely known that its fame and success
have been secured by the ability and untiring energy
of this gifted lady.   In the conduct of the business of
" Lorne House," its owner has been accustomed to
make almost monthly journeys to London and other
haunts of fashion, as well as to visit periodically the

more important manufacturing centres. Miss Mac-
Farlan Scott, as it were, steals away from the active
business of her warehouse and the duties of her
counting-house for a day or two now and again to rest
mind and body, which she sometimes does by
journeying to Loch Sloy, or by climbing the neighbouring hills (for a sprig of cloudberry) with such agility
that she has been described as one of the most
accomplished of lady mountaineers."

Neither of John's daughters married. Christina
pre-deceased her sister who, as we have stated, took up
housekeeping with her aunt, " The Chief." In the old
Edinburgh Directories we find the following entries :—

    1829-30.—Miss MacFarlane of that Ilk, 9 Dundas Street.
    1831-32.—Miss MacFarlane of that Ilk, 9 Dundas Street.
    1834-35.—Miss MacFarlane of that Ilk, 37 Heriot Row.

She died, probably in the Heriot Row house, on 12th
May, 1846, aged seventy-nine, and was interred in
Greyfriars' Churchyard, Edinburgh. The monument
bearing a well cut coat of arms, recording the deaths of
both the aunt and her niece, stands against the south-
west wall of the church. The full inscription it bears
is :—

IN MEMORY OF
JANET MACFARLAN,
DAUGHTER OF
WILLIAM MACFARLAN OF MACFARLAN, ESQ.,
DIED 2ND DECEMBER, 1821.
AND OF HER NIECE,
MARGARET ELIZABETH MACFARLAN,
WHO DIED 12TH MAY, 1846,
AGED 79 YEARS ;
BEING AT THE PERIOD OF HER DECEASE
THE LINEAL REPRESENTATIVE OF
THE ANCIENT AND HONOURABLE HOUSE
OF MACFARLAN OF THAT ILK.

SEPTS OF MACFARLANE.

ARRELL.

ARROL.

ALLAN (also ClanRanald).

ALLANSON (also Clan Ranald).

ALLANACH (also ClanRanald).

BARTHOLOMEW.

BARCLAY.

CAW.

GRIESCH (Aberdeen).

GRASSIE (Aberdeen).

GRASSICK (Montrose).

GRUAMACH.

GALLOWAY (Stirling).

KINNIESON.

KENNSON.

KINNISON.

MACALLAN (also ClanRanald, MacKay and Stewart).

MACAINDRA.

MACANDREW.

MACANDRO (of Dumbartonshire).

MACCAA.

MACCAUSE (Thomson).

MACCAW (also Stewart of Bute).

MACCONDEY.

MACEOIN.

MACEACHERN (also an ancient race of Kintyre and Criagnish)

MACERRACHER.

MACGAW.

MACGEOCH.

MACGREUSICH (also Buchanan).

MACINNES.

MACINSTALKER.

MACJOCK.

MACJAMES.

MACKINLAY.

MACNAIR (also McNaughton).

MACNEUR.

MACNUYER (also Buchanan and McNaughton).

MACNIDER.

MACNITER.

MACROB (also Gunn).

MACROBB.

MACWALTER.

MACWILLIAM (also Gunn).

MILLER (of Dumbartonshire).

MICHIE.

MONACH.

FARLANE.

ROBB.

STEWART.

STALKER.

WEAVER.

WILSON.

WEIR.

WILLIAMSON.

GALBRAITH.

LENNOX.

NAPIER.

CHAPTER XXIV.

SEPTS OF MACFARLANE.

"THE name of MacFarlane," writes Buchanan, "is very numerous both in the north and west Highlands, particularly in the counties of Dumbarton, Perth, Stirling and Argyle ; as also in the shires of Inverness and Moray and the western isles. Besides, there are a great many in the north of Ireland.

"There is also a vast number of descendants from, and dependents on, this surname and family, of other names, of which those of most account are a sept termed Allans or MacAllans, who are so called from Allan MacFarlane, their predecessor, a younger son of one of the Lairds of MacFarlane who went to the north and settled there, several centuries ago. This sept is not only very numerous, but also many of them are of very good account ; such as the families of Auchouachan, Balnengown, Druminn, etc. They reside mostly in Mar, Strathdon, and other northern counties.

"There are also MacNairs, MacEoins, MacErrachers, MacWilliams, MacAindras, MacNiters, MacInstalkers, MacJocks, Parlans, Farlans, Graumachs, Kinniesons etc., all which septs acknowledge themselves to be MacFarlanes, together with certain particular Septs of MacNayers, MacKinlays, MacRobbs, MacGreusichs, Smiths, Millers, Monachs and Weirs."

On another page we give a list of all the names we have been able to discover, attributed to MacFarlane. We are not prepared to vouch for the accuracy of this list. In the following pages is set forth such information as has reached us regarding particular names without making any claim to completeness.

In our list we have separated Galbraith, Lennox and Napier from the rest of the Septs, as we do not understand why these families should be included as MacFarlane. Galbraith was a separate and distinct family. Families of the name of Lennox must be either descended from the parent house of Lennox or from retainers of that family, while the only Napier connection is the marriage of a gentleman of that name with a daughter of Duncan, 8th Earl of Lennox. However, as these three are frequently given as Septs of MacFarlane, we include them here.

McALLAN.

As Buchanan remarks, the family of Allan or McAllan is one of considerable importance. Their progenitor, Allan MacFarlane, a younger son of one of the Chiefs of Arrochar, settled in the north of Scotland, and his sons, instead of taking the family patronymic, called themselves sons of Allan, just as, in another case, the sons of Thomas, younger son of Duncan, the 6th Chief, called themselves Thomas's sons instead of MacFarlane.

Allanson and Allanach are variants of MacAllan, adapted from the Gaelic, Aluinn, signifying illustrious.

The principal locations of the family are Mar, Strathdon, Glenbuchat and Glenmuick.

Macallan is an old place name in Aberdeenshire. The present parish of Knockando, in Moray, was originally called Macallan and was united to the parish of Knockando during the Regency of the Earl of Morton.

A Mr. J. Lindsay advances the startling statement that the name Parlane itself is really Allan. He writes :—

" The name Aluin (Ailin) or Parlan is purely Gaelic. Skene derives it from *al, alla, ail* or *aill,* a stone, rock, cliff, meaning the man of the cliff or rock; others from *ailean*, *ailen*, *ellen* and *allan*; a green plain, meadow; and from *fear*, a man, meaning the man of the green plain.. I rather favour the latter."

Mr. Lindsay's theory has only this justification, that the Celtic Parlan in Hebrew is Bartholomew, meaning " son of furrows," but, of course, Pharlain was not the founder of the family.

The following from *The Weekly . Scotsman*, by " Mac-an-t-Sionnaich," gives a summary of the ramifications of the name :—

" The Allans are a branch of a large Scottish family group, the MacAllans or Allans. The chief Highland branches were those of Aberdeenshire, Bute, Caithness, Dumbarton, Perth, and Ross.

" The name in Gaelic, Ailean, is derived from the early Irish Ailene, Adamnan's Ailenus.

" There were 11,578 Allans in Scotland in 1861.

" There are many forms of the Clan name—Allan, Allanach, Allanson, Alison, Allison, Callan, Callen, Callanach, MacAllan, MacAllen, and MacCallan. The Callans are a Bute family; the Allanachs belong to the Aberdeen Highlands and Strathspey; Callanach is an uncommon Appin form, while some Callens live at Dunoon. The Allansons and Allisons belong to the Lowlands, but they are no doubt of Highland or Celtic origin.

" According to tradition, the Clan Allan of Donside fought the Coutts, and were victors, at an early period. The MacAllans of Mar and Strathdon are descended from Allan MacFarlane, younger son of one of the Lairds of MacFarlane, who settled in Strathdon many centuries ago. His descendants were known as MacAllans, Allanich, or Clan Allan. Some of these MacAllans are alluded to by Nisbet (' System of Heraldry ') as of Lismurdie, Auchorrachan, Balnagown, Kirkton, and Markinch, etc.

" We find that ' The ancestor of the MacFarlanes of

Kirkton (Stirling) was George MacFarlane, of Markinch (Fife), second son to Andrew MacFarlane of that ilk, in the reign of James V. (See Chapter XXXII.). George, having sold the foresaid lands of Markinch, settled eventually in the north Highlands among his namesakes, the MacFarlanes, promiscuously called in the Irish (Gaelic) language M'Allans, Allanich, or Clan Allan, because of this descent from Allan MacFarlane. From him (George) are descended the families of Auchorrachan, Balnagown, and Lismurdie, etc., as also several others in Braemar and Strathspey.   His posterity continued in the North for several generations, until the time of Patrick MacFarlane, the fourth descendant in a direct line, who, returning again to the South, purchased the lands of Kirkton (Stirling) ' (History of Stirlingshire, v. 2, p. 100-1.). James M'Allane, in Dellaborar, Braemar, was prosecuted for ' remaining at the horn,' 1619 (R. of P.C.).   John Allan, in Delmucklachlie (Mar) was a resetter of outlawed MacGregors, 1636.

"The Allanachs of Strathdon are also apparently sprung from the MacFarlanes, ' Na Allanich,' Finlay Allenoch was a tenant in the lands of Innernete (Towie) in 1588. William Allanach, in Glenmuick, was prosecuted for resetting outlawed MacGregors, in 1636. There were Allanachs in Torrnonich, in 1660.   William Allanach, in Cattie, near Birse, 1671.   Allanachs in Muchrach, Strathspey, 1719.   There were four Allanachs in the Strathdon Volunteers in 1798, including Sergt. Duncan Allanach.   In 1903, there were two families in Glenbuchat, one at Torrancroy, and one at Upperton.   They are still to be found in Strathdon and Tarland.

"John MacAllan, in Alyth, was a follower of the Ogilvies of Clova, in 1585. . John MacAllan, in Enoch, Strathardle, and others were warned·not to harm the Robertsons of Straloch, in 1598.   Donald and Finlay MacAllan, in Easter Russachan, Menteith, were fined in 1612 for resetting outlawed MacGregors. Donald Allan, in Connachan, Glen Almond, was a prisoner in Edinburgh Tolbooth, with some MacGregors, in 1690— 'Baron' Finlay MacAllan, of Stramanane, 1506. Allan MacAllane obtained part of the lands of Langilwenach in 1506, which descended to his heirs. Robert Allan disponed Easgechraggan and Glenbuy to Sir Dugald Stewart in 1669. Ninian Allan was officer of the Castle of Rothesay in 1681. There are still many Allans and Callans in Bute.

" There are many Allans and MacAllans in Caithness, and these are probably sprung from William M'Allan, descendant of Ferchard of Melness, the physician, about 1379. ' William M'Allan sold the Small Isles to Sir Donald M'Kay of Strathnavor. There is abounding evidence in various wadsett charters of this period that the MacAllans were MacKays, the former surname being a patronymic, and quite in keeping with the custom of the time.' (See *Celtic Monthly*, April, 1910).

" Finlay MacAllan appears in the chanonry, Ross, 1578 ; Thomas Allan, servitor of Munro of Tarrell, Ross, 1607 ; Finlay MacAllan, in Tain, 1628 ; John MacAllan, Ulleray, N. Uist, was a tenant on the MacDonald estate, 1718 ; Gilfelan (Gilfillan) M'Allan and others were accused of the slaughter of Gillaspy MacClery (now Leckie), at Stirling Assizes, 1477 ; John, younger, and John MacAllan, elder, were native tanners at Port of Roisdo (Rosdhu), Dumbarton, 1621.

" The surname Alison or Allison is no doubt derived from Allanson. Some authorities have suggested ' son of Alice,' but this origin is most unlikely. Thomas Allesoun of Lochtoune, Scone, 1587 ; Archibald Allasoun M'Arthur, Argyll, 1590 ; James Allasson, in Ledcamroch, Balvie, Dumbarton, 1671.

" Allsoun was another ancient form of the name.

" Branch Tartans.—MacFarlane—Allan, Allanach, MacAllan, MacAllen, of Aberdeen and Banff.

" MacKay—Allan, MacAllan of Caithness.

" Stewart of Bute—Allan, Callan, Callen, MacAllan, MacCallan of Bute.

" The following cannot be allocated with certainty :— Allanson, Alison, Allison, and Callanach."

ARROL.

Arrol or Arrell is said to be a Dumbartonshire family of the Sept of MacFarlane of Kepnoch. The name itself is derived from the place-name of Errol, in Perthshire (Arroll, 1660).

Many of this name lived on the MacFarlane and Colquhoun lands in Dumbartonshire, in the 16th and 17th centuries.

Duncan Errole, minister of Luss, 1590.

Thomas Arroll, in Arochiebeg, Dumbartonshire, under the MacFarlane, and John Errol, in Cashlie, were fined in 1614, for resetting members of the Clan Gregor.

Duncan Arrell, cordiner, in Drumlegark, was put to the horn, in 1619, with the MacFarlanes of Kepnoch for raiding (Reg. of P.C.).

Robert Arroll, Dalnair, Lennox, 1592.

Thomas Errole, in Blairoule, and others, retainers of Stewart of Ardvorlik, raided the lands of Cunningham of Drumquhassill, 1592.

John Arrell, servitor of the Laird of Tullichewne, 1569.

Sir William Arrol, a famous 20th century engineer.

BARCLAY.

As to this name being a Sept of MacFarlane, our informant is Malcolm MacFarlane, the well known Gaelic authority, who writes :—" It will surprise you to learn that many of the Ulster Barclays are MacFarlanes in the Gaelic. I had evidence of this many years ago, and could hardly accept it, but the case is as I state."

MacGreusach.

This name means son of the " greusaich " or shoe-maker—from which we have the Lowland Souter.

MacInstalker.

The meaning of this name is obvious—the son of the stalker—now represented by Stalker only. In 1565 Neil, son of John Malloch (the Mallochs dwelt in the district of Rannoch) was one of the persons employed by the Government to take vengeance on the murderers (MacInstalkers) of the son of MacGregor, Dean of Lismore.

MacNiter.

MacNiter is a phonetic representation of " Mac-an-fhigheadair "—son of the weaver.

MacNair.

" The MacNairs of Lennox," writes Fionn, " now go by the name of Weir."

The legend which gave origin to the " Mac-an-Oighres " or MacNairs of Lennox is that of " The Piebald Horse." Fionn's version is, as follows :—

" In the reign of James III. of Scotland, the Laird of MacFarlane was slain at the battle of Sauchieburn, Stirling, in the year 1488, leaving a widow, who was an English lady, the mother of one son ; he also left a son by his first wife, who was his heir ; but this son and heir had the misfortune to be proud, vain, silly, and a little weak-minded. His half-brother was possessed of a beautiful grey horse, which had been given to him by some of his mother's relatives. The elder brother was about to set out for Stirling, and was very desirous of riding this horse, wishing, as the young chief, to make a good appearance. The step-mother refused the loan of the animal, alleging, as her reason for so doing, her fear that it would not be safely brought back. Her denial only made the young man more persistent. Finally a written agreement was drawn up and signed by the heir, in which he promised to forfeit to his half-brother his lands of Arrochar, in case the horse was not safely returned.

"The step-mother bribed the groom in attendance to poison the horse on the second day from home, and the estate accordingly went to the younger brother. The Clan refused to receive the latter as their Chief, but combined to acknowledge the elder brother as such, though not possessed of the lands of Arrochar. Some years later, by special Act of Parliament, these lands were restored to the rightful heir. Old people in Lennox referred to certain MacFarlanes as 'Sliochd an eich bhain,' descendants of the white horse, being those who followed the half-brother in contradistinction to those who followed the heir, or 'Clann an Oighre,' as they called themselves." (Also see Chapter X.).

Another writer makes the following remarks about the MacNairs :—

"This name is derived from at least three sources, namely, the Lennox Sept, connected with the MacFarlanes, the Argyleshire Sept, connected with the MacNaughtons, and the Ross-shire Sept, connected with the MacKenzies. Those of the Lennox were originally MacFarlanes."

Dr. MacBain says :—"The Perthshire Sept appears in documents as M'Inayr, 1468 ; Macnayr, 1390 ; which is explained Mac-an-Oighre, son of the heir. The MacNairs of Cowal, etc., anglicise their name to Weir. These MacNairs are said to have been originally MacNaughtons. There were McNuirs in Cowal, 1685 ; and a John Maknewar, in Dunoon, 1546. The Mac-Nuyers of the Lennox also now are known by the name of Weir. Of the Gairloch Sept, MacNair, Gaelic, Mac-an-uidhar (this is condensed into M'In-uir) for MacIain uidhir son of dun (*odhar*), John ; such is the source of the Ross-shire branch. Other facts point to another origin, Mac-an-Fuibhir, the stranger's son."

Mr. J. W. MacNair Wallace has made some investigations into the origin of the name MacNair, and gave a summary of his collections in *The Oban Times* of 16th January, 1909.

"In the Exchequer Rolls of Scotland, the name of 'M'Noyare, maro de Menteth' appears in the rent roll of the Earldom of Mar, and in the accounts of the Chamberlain of Monteith we find 'Malcolme Mac-Macnoyare,' or 'Macnoyar.' In 1454 the name of 'M'Noyare de Menteth, mari de Down, et mari de Strogartenay' appears. In 1456 he appears again as 'M'Noyare,' and in the same year one 'Gillaspy M'Nare' is mentioned as having been put in irons at Kyrkcuchbrith, being released in 1457, his name then spelled 'Maknare.' In 1457 there is mention of a 'M'Nayr, inhabitans terras' of Duchray, in the Strathearn and Menteith accounts, while in the rentals of the Crown lands of the Barony of Downe in 1480 we find the names of 'Donaldo M'Nayr,' 'Dovok Maknair,' and 'Johanni Maknair.' Curiously, the last-mentioned has his name spelled twice as 'Maknair' and twice as 'Maknain,' in the rolls, between 1486 and 1492. In the latter rolls we also find a 'Donaldo M'Hubir,' otherwise 'Donaldi Makhubir,' and 'Donaldo M'Ubir'; can this be the same as the ''Donaldo M'Nayr' above mentioned? In the same rentals of Doune, between 1492 and 1500 are 'Donaldo M'Nvyr' and 'Andree M'Nvyr,' as well as a 'Johanni Smyth.' In 1521 in the Rentals of Menteith, Parkland de Down, we have 'Elizabeth Maknair,' and in 1532 mention is made of William Hamilton of 'Maknaristoun,' auditor of Exchequer. In the Menteith accounts also, in a rental dated at Halyruidhous in 1574, we find a 'Donaldum M'Newer.'

"In the Register of the Great Seal of Scotland for the period between 1424 and 1513, 'Rob. Macnare' appears as a witness to a charter, but between 1546 and 1580 the name assumes the forms of 'M'Nair,'

' Maknair,' ' Makynnair,' ' M'Kynnair,' and ' Makkyn-
nair,' and in a charter of the lands of Menteith in 1554
there is a tenant ' Joh. Maknoyare.'   In a charter dated
in 1576 at the ' Palatium S. Crucis,' mention is made of
a ' Duncano M'Kynnair in Dunkeld.'   In a confirmation
of a charter in 1686 appears ' Roberti Maknair, canonici
Dunkelden,' as well as ' Johanni M'Nair ' and ' Jacobi
M'Nair.' ' Robert Maknair ' also appears in 1697.
I should, perhaps, add that the ' Robert Makynnair '
was ' rector de Assent ' in 1548.

"From the Calendar of Scottish Papers we find that
in February, 1568, ' Arche Macnare ' is one of those
then attached to, or attendant on, Queen Mary. The
same list of attendants gives the name of one ' Oduar
of Tralltrow.'   In the papers for 1298 the names of
' Gillespic M'Enri ' and ' Cuthbert M'Enri ' are given
as residenters in Galloway. Is there any connection
here ?

"In 1605 the Register of the Privy Council of
Scotland mentions ' Patrick M'Nair,' in Bray of Cluny,
' Johne M'Nedar,' in Mayboll, and ' Alexander M'Nedar'
in Drumnoir;   while in 1584 we have a ' Johne
M'Knedar,' burgess of Air; in 1585 an ' Oswald
M'Knedar ' and a ' Johnne M'Nedar ' ' Johnne
M'Nedair ' appears in Register of the Privy Council at
Holyrood-house as a witness to a bond in 1589, and
' Johnne M'Nir elder,' in 1591. In 1592 among those
charged to appear to answer certain charges, and
denounced as rebels for non-appearance, are ' M'Noder
in Strogarne, M'inair, Carfing; Johnne M'innair at
the Port of Locharne ; Allister Moir M'indeir, servant
to Alexander Steuart in Auldverik; and John Dow
M'Neir.'   Can this ' M'Noder in Strogarne ' be of the
same family as the ' M'Noyare de Menteth, mari de
Strogartenay' in 1454? If so, this rather favours the
' d ' of ' Odhar.'   To conclude these registers, in 1595,
' Donald M'Noyer, servant ' at Mildaying, is mentioned.

"The only mention of the name in the Lang charters

is between 1566 and 1582, and is of a Sir Duncan Maknair, alias M'Nair, notary, and treasurer of Dunkeld.

"In conclusion may I mention 'Nigello Fabro' and 'Patricium Fabrum,' both of Tarbert, whose names appear in the Exchequer Rolls in 1264; and we also have 'Willelmi Fabri de Lochrys,' alias 'Luchris,' in 1353 and 1387. This looks like Professor Mackinnon's 'fuibbir.'

"In Adam's 'Clans of Scotland,' the MacNairs and MacNeurs are given as Septs of the MacFarlanes, and the MacNuyers as a Sept of the Macnaughtons. This points to two quite separate families."

Mr. Wallace at that time was seeking information in regard to reference made in *The Oban Times* to the MacNairs in Cowal in 1685, Maknewar in Dunoon in 1546, and MacNuyer in Inverness in 1681, also MacInayre, Loch Tay, in 1438, MacNayr (Raid of Angus) in 1390, and MacNewar in Dunoon Parish in 1546.

ROBB.

There is a considerable difference of opinion as to whether or not Robb is entitled to rank as a Sept of MacFarlane. We have ourselves, no definite opinion on the subject. E. W. R. in *The Weekly Scotsman*, wrote:—"This name is of Norman descent and is a Royal name. Their crest is a naked arm holding up a crown wreathed in laurel. They are connected with the Clan MacFarlane and wear their tartan."

Writing to the Hon. Secy. of the Society of The Clan MacFarlane, Mr. M. D. Ross, of Edinburgh, on the other hand, remarked:—"No reliance ought to be placed on traditional pedigrees in the case of so famous a Clan as MacFarlane, and the officials should stick out for the real Chief representing the old line, or, otherwise, appoint a president till the real heir of the race is found. . . . . . The enclosed cutting (E. W. R.'s remarks quoted above) shews what absurd views find their way into print. The Robbs do not wear the MacFarlane tartan."

A Mr. Robb bore out Mr. Ross, and Mr. J. Lindsay wrote in reply :—

" Mr. Wm. Robb's assumptions seem out of place, in view of the fact that I have often heard of the Robbs belonging to the M'Farlane Clan, in Lanarkshire. If he looks up Johnston's ' History of the Clans,' he will find this opinion corroborated. The name comes from Robert, Robb being the Scottish form of the name. Robert is said to be a Teutonic personal name of great antiquity, introduced into Britain about the time of the Conquest. Robertus is frequently found in the ' Domestic Book.' Besides having itself become a surname, it has given rise to a great many others, as Roberts, Robarts, Robertson, Robins, Robbins, Robinson, Robbie, Robison, Robeson, Robb, Robson, Roby. It has also taken the form of Fitz-Robert, and in Wales, of Ap-Robert and Ap-Robyn, now contracted to Probert and Probyn. Variants are Dobb and Hobb, from the former of which we get Dobbs, Dobby, Dobbie, Dobson, Dabson, Dobbin, Dobbins, Dobinson ; and from the latter, Hobbs, Hobbes, Hobson, Hobbins, Hobkins, Hopkins, Hopkinson, and Hoby. In the olden times all, no matter what name they had, had to be dependents of some Sept or Clan for their own safety. Clan MacFarlane has a fair list of other names than its own, such as Gruamach, Griesck, Kinnieson, Lennox, MacAindra, M'Allan, M'Caa, M'Cause, M'Caw, M'Eoin, M'Erracher, M'Gaw, M'Geoch, M'Nair, M'Rob, M'Robb, M'Walter, M'William, Michie, Napier, Parlane, Stalker, Weaver, Weir. These are not all, but they let us see how our ancestors had to bind themselves together for defence."

McWILLIAM.

McWilliam is another name in dispute. Mr. H. D. McWilliam, writing in *The Celtic Monthly*, says :—

" The writer is aware that his patronymic is to be found in works relating to the clans as a Sept name of the Clan MacFarlane only, suggesting to the uninitiated, at least, that all McWilliams belong to that Clan. If any one chooses to write to a tartan warehouse for a pattern of McWilliam tartan, he will be promptly furnished with one of the Clan MacFarlane. There could be no greater delusion, and it may indeed be that there are no *present day* McWilliams connected with that Clan, as it was usual for Septs after two or three generations to drop the patronymic and re-assume the Clan name, and seeing that the authority is Buchanan of Auchmar, who wrote some two centuries ago, the patronymic may well have subsequently fallen into disuse by the MacFarlanes. The writer could cite a number of instances of the use of the patronymic in connection with different Clans in the course of the last two or three centuries where it was afterwards superseded by the Clan name."

(Here follows over twenty references to McWilliams in Glenlivet).

" In Glenlivet," further remarks Mr. McWilliam, " in the parish of Inveravon, Banffshire, there were, in the 17th and 18th centuries, families distinguished by the name of Macphersons, alias McWillie or M'Cullie, certain descendants of which, in the present day, are known as McWilliam and McWillie. The ancestors of the latter, on removal from Glenlivet towards the end of the 17th century, appear to have discontinued the use of the name MacPherson, this being apparently in conformity with the practice of Highlanders in similar cases when removing to a Lowland district. There they would have of necessity to choose one name and adhere to it. Certain families remaining in the glen, however, continued for a century later to be called by both names, and it would appear that they, in all probability, finally adhered to Macpherson.

M

"But although the families which left the Glen in the 17th century also left what may be called their Clan name behind them, their descendants, for the most part, retain traditions to this day indicative of a Macpherson origin. One of these is to the effect that a McWillie, resident in the parish of Cabrach, at the '45', sent a substitute attired in Macpherson tartan to fight for Prince Charlie. Another tradition is that the McWillies (now McWilliams) who settled on the estate of Grant of Ballindalloch about 1743, were asked by Macpherson of Invereshie on his succeeding to Ballindalloch in 1806, to assume (or resume) the name of Macpherson. This laird, it appears, had the reputation among old Badenoch seanachies of being wonderfully conversant with the history, traditions, genealogies, etc., of his own clan, so that if he believed these McWillies to be real Macphersons there could be nothing more natural than that he should urge them, as a Chief of his name, to re-assume their old surname.

"In these days, when one sees so many enquiries as to the particular Clan to which persons belong, it has occurred to the writer that the insertion of these notes might prove helpful to others who, like the writer, are saddled with a patronymic which has prevailed in many Clans."

"Wilson is a form of Williamson or MacWilliam.

WEIR.

As has already been suggested, the name Weir is an anglicised form of MacNair. Other explanations of its origin are :—

"This name is derived from a local circumstance, to wit, one who resided by or near to a weir (on a river). It is fairly plentiful in Scotland. Major Weir, of evil fame, was a well known Edinburgh figure, and in 1794 a Weir had a museum of natural history at No. 16 Princess Street. .Crest—a demi-horse, arg. Motto— Nihil verius ('Nothing more true ').

"·The Weirs are an old Lanarkshire family, there having been landed proprietors of that name for many generations in that district, although the family is no longer there. I have been told, though I have no proof of the fact,that the name was originally De Vere. It may therefore be of Norman descent. The crest is a hand upright holding a wreath of olive. Motto— In utriumque paratus ('Prepared for anything')."

Finally, in an autograph letter from the Rev. John Weir, St. James' Manse, Forfar, occurs the following, which, from a romantic standpoint, we like best of all :—

"The Weirs are believed to be a branch of the MacFarlanes, the tradition being that more than 150 years ago there were two young men, brothers, understood to be sons of the head of the Clan at Arrochar. They quarrelled, both being in love with the same lady. The younger ran his sword into the body of the elder, and, fearing he had killed him, fled over the hills. Finding himself pursued, and seeing men smelting or forging metal in a rude way, he appealed to them to protect or hide him. They hid him in a pit, and directed the pursuers to hasten beyond where he was hidden. The young man became 'feurin,' which, in Gaelic, is a forger (of iron). The word 'feurin' is said to have been gradually changed to Weir—F transmuted into W."

MacJock.

This name is the modern Jackson, *i.e.*, Jock's son.

MacCondy.

"Amongst the prairie scouts who made civilisation possible in the great West," writes R. Graham Fergusson, "the McCondys were a Sept of the Clan MacFarlane. The Mac was usually dropped, as in the case of Elias Bean, the greatest of them all."

BV - #0090 - 091222 - C0 - 229/152/12 - PB - 9781330637593 - Gloss Lamination